To my wife Hazel and daughter Emma for helping me to w

SAGA OF THE GOODWINS

David Chamberlain

By the same author:
FORGOTTEN SHIPWRECKS OF THE DOWNS
A HERITAGE FROM THE GOODWINS
THE GOODWIN SANDS MAN-OF-WAR
TALES FROM AROUND THE GOODWIN SANDS

Published by BEACHES BOOKS
01304 362744

ISBN O-9548439-2-4

CONTENTS

INTRODUCTION

Over the years it has been estimated there have been at least 2000 shipwrecks on and around the Goodwin Sands and the total number of lost lives is incalculable. The capricious sea has no prejudice as to whom she takes. Even the most experienced will fall foul of her moods. The trauma of being shipwrecked has constantly haunted many of those who were lucky enough to be saved. For some the ordeal would be too much and the nightmares would only disperse with death. However, men will still risk their own lives to try and save others.

Prior to the twentieth-century the Downs, Goodwin Sands and shipwrecks were once the life-blood of Deal and the town's arteries were her longshoremen. With up to 400 ships at any one time at anchor in the Downs, the local boatmen made a living by conveying ships' stores to those vessels. These stores comprised of ropes, tackle, food, water, ale, clothing and anything else that was needed aboard a ship which was short on supplies. Ashore, the mills, chandlers, slop-shops, butchers, bakers and every other kind of manufacturers were making a handsome profit from the shipping companies.

Deal longshoremen's skill at launching and beaching their boats in difficult conditions were well known. Nevertheless, this dexterity came at a price. It was noted that in very bad weather even Nelson had to pay the sum of 15 guineas to an intrepid boatman, to be ferried back to his ship that was anchored in the Downs.

The heaviest work was carried out by the forepeak luggers. These fine two-masted sea boats were up to 40 feet in length, with some weighing 20 tons. They would have a large part of the foredeck covered which could accommodate a crew of six to eight men. With a small stove installed, they could cruise about the anchorage in almost any weather for days on end. From the forepeak aft, the craft would have an open work deck, upon which small cargoes or salvage could be carried.

These rapacious men in their luggers could strip a shipwreck in situ of her masts, rigging and even the copper sheathing which covered her hull below the waterline. Anything of value or usage would be brought ashore before the hulk disintegrated on the Sands. They were termed as 'hovelers', the origin of which has been much debated and questioned. Perhaps a simple answer was that they were 'hoverers' and the word has been slightly altered with local colloquial use.

The luggers' travels would not be limited solely to hovering in the Downs; they sailed further distances, up and down the coast, until a job could be found. Again this work could be diverse; from giving advice and help, taking off mail, providing pilots and taking out anchors and cables to ships that were in need.

Another type of local vessel was the galley, which needed less manpower to launch. These all-purpose, clinker-built craft were renowned for their speed and sailing qualities. Up to 30 feet in length with a narrow beam and a large dipping lugsail, they could out run any sailing vessel of the same size. Once more it was the proficiency of the Deal boatmen which attained the deftness of these light, shallow draught boats. The men had to carry half a ton of shingle ballast, which had to be moved to the weather side at each change of tack. When wind conditions were light they were equipped with five rowing thwarts, from where the oarsmen could propel the craft through a calm sea at a rate of knots. These small workboats were the saviour of many a shipwrecked mariner.

It was not surprising that the prosperity of Deal and her boatmen peaked throughout the Napoleonic Wars. The breach of water between the foreshore and the awaiting ships was in constant use and stores and troops were being steadily ferried out to the naval fleet stationed in their own anchorage. The Admiralty's naval yard was thriving, making and repairing ships' tackle, and employed many local craftsmen. For numerous officers and their wives prior to embarkation, accommodation became very scarce. Needless to say the public houses and inns did a roaring trade.

Unfortunately a darker side to the honest, but lucrative, boatmen's trade evolved – namely smuggling. After the wars this nefarious traffic continued and increased; there was always a market for French brandy that the sought-after English gold coins could buy.

The treacherous Goodwin Sands continued to claim ships and lives, and only a small relief was brought about when the Elder Brethren of the Trinity started to mark the sand banks with light vessels in the early 1800s. The lifeboats were introduced by the National Lifeboat Institution in 1865, and there were three based on the beaches of Deal, Walmer and Kingsdown. Unfortunately it was by this time that the community of Deal was starting to lose its revenue from the sea.

With the coming of steam ships the longshoremen were no longer needed. Anchor chains tended not to part, as did hemp, and the two-cylinder compound engine could push a vessel into the very teeth of a gale. Nevertheless, there were always boatmen aplenty to man the lifeboats and their brave exploits were constantly in the newspapers of the time – which kept the knowledge of Deal and the Goodwin Sands at the forefront of the British public.

Hopefully, we will never witness a return of the Goodwins catastrophes which were commonplace in the past. Optimistically the author anticipates that this book will reflect on some of the hardships that our forbearers suffered in their struggle against the saga of the Goodwins.

David Chamberlain 2006

Guardians of the Mary Hougham Almshouses, Deal

There were no survivors

THE SECRET OF THE SANDS

Captain Daniel Ronzieres was not overtly distrustful; he was merely obeying company rules as the boxes, containing thousands of silver bars, were stowed neatly and securely in his cabin. Along with the bullion, over 36,000 silver coins in similar boxes joined the hoard. As each chest was being checked against the manifest, the rest of the less valuable cargo was being loaded into the holds of the Dutch East India Company (VOC) ship *Rooswijk*.

The Dutch port of Texel had been busy with other VOC ships, although the three-year-old *Rooswijk* was deemed to be the largest. Most of the cargo that was being stowed below her decks was mundane. Sheet copper, masonry blocks, cases of sabres and other weapons were being taken to establish and maintain the forces and buildings in the Dutch East India Company's headquarters at Batavia, South East Asia.

In that year of 1740, it seemed that the Eastern Continent had no need for European goods. However, *their* spices, porcelain and silks were in demand and fetched excellent prices. It was because of these circumstances that the VOC ships had to carry vast amounts of specie, with which to purchase their produce.

The ingots of silver were originally mined from Spanish held Mexico, and then sold to the Dutch to be melted down into four-pound bars with the Amsterdam VOC stamp upon each one. The ingots would have been converted in Batavia – now Jakarta – into Javanese currency with the rest shipped off to Siam (Thailand) and Bengal to be made into their local coinage.

Inside some of the bonded boxes were thousands of silver eight reales, along with roughly cut and stamped cobs. These coins – about the size of the British crown – were known and used throughout the world as 'pieces of eight'. The silver content, which was also mined and minted in Spanish Mexico, contained a regular 26.5 grams of .903 fine silver.

As the hatches on *Rooswijk's* cargo holds were covered with canvas and secured with rope, Captain Ronzieres thoughts were with the voyage ahead. They were not of the fear from pirates or privateers – as the ship carried a formable amount of cannon and a crew of 250 men, which included soldiers – but of the adverse weather.

It was the beginning of January and a bitterly cold north-east wind had set in. As they

Piece of eight

made sail on the 8th the wind increased to gale-force. The relatively calm confines of Texel were soon behind them as the off-shore wind rapidly reached storm force. All that day and night they fought against the elements. When darkness fell the following night, further vision was obliterated by a blizzard. Daniel Ronzieres's men found working the pitching and rolling 850 ton ship extreme and hazardous. They were continually making sail changes to the vessel as she tacked back and forth making for the open sea and away from the shallow Dutch shoals.

While the night wore on conditions became worse and navigation impossible. In the thick weather Ronzieres had lost his bearings as the ship was being driven further westward by the wind. He calculated that he could not beat up against it and reduced his sails to a minimum. The captain had no idea what part of the English Channel they were in, however the constant sounding of the lead showed that he had plenty of water under the keel. He also considered that it was too deep for the ship to anchor and wait for the storm to abate.

Most of the soldiers were suffering from acute nausea and trying to hold on to anything that was secure in their restricted quarters. The cooking fires had been extinguished soon after they had left port and freezing conditions now permeated throughout the vessel. Those below decks were becoming hypothermic and, with sea-sickness, were losing the will to live. The seamen were too busy to succumb to this malady and merely cursed the weather – although the least courageous of them were starting to realise the desperate state that their ship was in. Apart from her billowing sails the rest of the *Rooswijk* was covered in snow, building up in small drifts on the windward side of her bulwarks. Footprints on the deck from the crew were soon covered, as the ship careered along with the storm.

As the vessel ran up on to the Goodwin Sands, the crew and troops felt the ship jolt to a halt and then start to slew uncontrollably, beam on to the heavy seas. Immediately, tumultuous waves overwhelmed her and giant seas crashed down upon the deck, sweeping away any persons that were still standing. The masts were wrenched out of the steps in her keelson, splintering and ripping up the deck. Within minutes the heavily laden Dutch East Indiaman was gripped by the sand and started to break up, as the massive seas pulverized her to pieces. The deaths of the entire crew and troops were almost instantaneous. They were drowned in the freezing conditions and their screams for salvation unheard.

Morning arrived with the storm still blowing. Deal boatmen, unable to launch their boats in the heavy surf, wandered the beach in search of any scraps that the onshore wind had blown in and it was soon evident to the men that there had been a shipwreck in the night. However, the pieces of washed up timbers were so broken that they could not identify the unfortunate vessel. When one man came upon a chest, surging about in the surf, he eagerly risked becoming drenched as he snatched it from the waves.

On opening the chest, a look of disappointment clouded his face. In the casket were vast amounts of waterlogged letters written in a foreign hand. When the honest fellow handed the mail in to the authorities, the name of the ill-fated ship was then discovered. The loss, to the Dutch company, was a great one, financially, as well as in human terms.

In the year 1998, Ken Welling, a Cambridgeshire carpenter, had worked out an area on the Goodwin Sands where the wreck of the *Rooswijk* might have been. This was achieved after many hours of research and deduction from English newspapers of the eighteenth-century and Dutch archives. In the years that followed Welling searched, with the limited amount of equipment he could tow from his 23ft boat, on and around the hostile waters of the Goodwin Sands. His quest would always be fraught with danger; as when he found wreckage protruding from the seabed, he would dive upon it alone. With the shifting sandbanks of the Goodwins he knew there was always going to be the chance that the wreck would never reappear.

Eventually in the summer of 2004, Ken found what he had been looking for. It started off as just another bottom target on the echo sounder, although his magnetometer showed that there was a vast amount of ferrous metal causing the machine to peak. Whilst diving on these new wrecks he was always hopeful, nevertheless, he was used to disappointments. Over the years he had found many old rotting timbers on the seabed which he could eliminate from his search. When he found some cannons amongst the timbers, he was soon to realise that this was a wreck of status. Further exploration showed that there were chests, although worn, still intact. When he came upon one with its top off, he saw the glint of silver. At last his vision had been fulfilled.

During 1798, the Dutch East India Company (VOC) was taken over by the Dutch Government who, to this day, is still the legal owners of all treasures that were lost from the VOC ships. Ken made contact with a representative and, in total secrecy, they arranged for the bullion to be recovered.

Through the dive season of 2005, from July until late August, the 500 ton diving support vessel *Terschelling*, appeared on the sky line off Deal. The *Terschelling* was skippered by Nigel J Boston, who, along with his team of professional divers, was very skilled in the art of recovering old and valuable relics – in the past the vessel had spent numerous periods on the wreck-site of the *Mary Rose*. Also aboard was the eminent underwater archaeologist Alex Hildred and it was she who oversaw and catalogued over a thousand artefacts. Amongst these objects were the personal items of the crew; from the officers mess deck, pewter plates, glass wine goblets and a pewter mustard pot – with a spoon still in it. A huge copper cauldron from the galley and fifty muskets from the Master at Arms' cabin were rescued. For Alex, all these artefacts were making a social statement from the eighteenth-century.

Although the vessel could be seen from Deal and Ramsgate there was, apart from a few inquisitive fishermen, little interest in her goings on. It was certainly unknown, to the majority, that she was reclaiming a vast fortune of silver, which had lain on the Goodwins for 265 years.

Four months later some of the treasure was handed to Holland's government finance minister, Joop Wijn. He accepted it, along with many artefacts destined for Dutch museums, aboard the Dutch Royal Navy frigate *De Ruyter*, at Plymouth. Due to the tragedy in 1740, the silver bullion never reached its destination, yet was not completely lost when, over a quarter of a millennium later, the Goodwins released its centuries old secret location – thanks to the determination and dedication of diver, Ken Welling.

Terschelling recovering boxes of silver from the Goodwin Sands

9

The *Loanda's* holds were stacked with thousands of cases of alcohol

HIDDEN SILVER?

As the first rays of the early summer sun attempted to warm the seawater in the Channel and North Sea, a dense fog formed. It was a thick, wet, dripping fog that shrouded the ships and covered the lookouts with shimmering moist cobwebs on their hair and beards. The continuous blasts of the steam ships' foghorns came from every quarter in a cacophony of confusion.

The first ship to collide, on Saturday 30th May, 1908, was the Spanish vessel, *Bermeo,* with the British steamer *Queenswood.* Next, just after midnight, was the *Junona,* with the Elder Dempster liner *Loanda.*

Being a 1,000 tons heavier, the Russian steam ship *Junona's* bow had no problem piercing the *Loanda's* port side, near number two hold.

The *Loanda* was a fine vessel. She had 44 first-class cabins and 14 second class. On a regular run to Africa she always had full cargo holds and an exclusive passenger list. The Empire was being exploited by most white nations and the coast of Africa had a lot to offer – eventually making many men rich.

At Rotterdam, the ship had been loaded up with 6,000 cases of gin and the same again with rum and schnapps. Along with several thousand cases of gunpowder, other minor trinkets such as clay pipes and chinaware were checked off on the cargo list.

Much of the cargo that was loaded into the holds of the Elder Dempster vessel was manifested, however, there was possibly a lot that was not recorded.

The missionaries on the West Coast of Africa knew their jobs were going to be that much harder after the *Loanda* had docked. They knew that this consignment of alcohol was not only for the colonists but would be used for trade amongst the natives. It would buy tusks of ivory that would then be exported back to Europe. The greed of personal fortunes outweighed the disruption and addiction that rum and gin would bring.

A rumour was spread that the ship also carried £98,000 of uninsured silver in the form of bars and African shillings. These were allegedly stowed in a cabin portside forward and below the bridge – which had been turned into a strong room. What this bullion – if it was onboard – would have been used for, can only be speculated on.

On impact, the *Loanda's* engine-room was filled with water and she started to settle. When the lights failed, seamen and passengers mustered on to the boat-deck and hastily launched the lifeboats. The fog had cleared to a mist and other vessels stood by the sinking ship. Twenty-one of the *Loanda* crew were transferred from their drifting lifeboat on to the Norwegian

A porthole from the *Loanda*

steamer *Hildur* and, with her best speed, she made for Dover.

Not wanting to enter the harbour, the *Hildur* once more transferred the men on to a passing smack, *Diana*. It was this sailing vessel that landed the rescued sailors and alerted the authorities to the collision.

The two Dover Harbour tugs, *Lady Crundall* and *Lady Vita* had only just dispatched the other collision damaged *Queenswood* safely in the harbour. Within the hour they were notified that their services were once again needed, this time for the sinking *Loanda*.

They found the strickened ship five miles off the East Goodwins and surrounded by other steamships and sailing craft. The Dublin steamer, *City of Hamburg,* had unsuccessfully made several attempts to tow the *Loanda*, but had now given up on the arrival of the experts.

Both of the tugs surveyed the situation before they made a tow secure. The vessel was very low in the water, almost awash, nevertheless, she seemed fairly stable. Sea conditions were calm and the *Loanda's* captain and officers were standing-by their ship in a lifeboat. When the vast value of the *Loanda's* cargo was explained to the tug masters, they realised that a successful effort would be financially rewarding.

The *Lady Crundall* and *Lady Vita* piled on steam, encouraging the semi-sunken ship to get some way on her. Slowly the *Loanda* responded to their endeavours. Hours went by and as they rounded the *South Goodwin* lightship more vessels came out to escort them into Dover.

Just off St Margaret's Bay and three miles short of the harbour, the *Loanda* suddenly began to sink by her stern.

Small china bowl found in her hold

Pandemonium surrounded the scene. Ten men were tipped into the sea from the ship's lifeboat, that was tied up alongside the wreck, and were swiftly rescued. Another five longshoremen in a galley from Deal had to be saved when their boat was lost in the vortex of the sinking ship. Hatch covers, life-rings and debris covered the area where the vessel had once been. Disappointed and downhearted the tugs and crew made their way back to Dover.

Within eyesight of their goal, a fortune had slipped out of their grasp.

Meanwhile, the *Junona* could not continue her voyage to St Petersburg, because of the extensive damage to her bow that she had maintained in the collision with the *Loanda*.

She limped up the Thames on the following day, to put in for repairs. Whilst anchoring up, she managed to further collide with the barque *Berean*. A crewmember off the *Loanda*, who was unexplainably aboard the *Junona*, was glad to disembark at the Port of London.

Salvage was attempted on the wreck of the *Loanda*, however the strong tides made work difficult. When the weather took a turn for the worst, quantities of bottles were washed out of her holds. When they were cast up alongshore at St Margaret's Bay, the locals quickly devoured the contents before the coastguards could stop them. It was recorded that on the days when the square bottles of gin were strewn along the foreshore, so were the inhabitants in recumbent forms. One old lady died on the beach of alcohol poisoning.

As the months went by, there were no more efforts made on the wreck. Intensive beachcombing in the neighbourhood of St Margaret's Bay was only practised subsequent to a northerly storm. After many frustrated searches

Gin and Schnapps were a favourite

with nothing found, apart from driftwood, even the locals got fed up and forgot about her.

When, late in the 1970s, the *Loanda* was first discovered by the scuba divers, they thought they had found an underwater supermarket. Racks and cases of bottles in all shapes and sizes lay in the wrecks rusting holds – although the contents were undrinkable. Brass portholes littered the seabed where they had 'popped' away from the steel hull. Needless to say it became a very popular dive.

Over the years, divers became more adventurous and explored deeper into the hulk. They found ornate clay pipes and delicate china bowls, unbroken and still in their packing cases. Eventually, three divers brought the wreck off her insurers and made some endeavour to salvage the remaining cargo. They still allowed recreational divers to visit the wreck, nevertheless they insisted that it must be on 'a look but don't touch' basis.

A salver-lid from the 1st class passengers dining-room

If the alleged £98,000 of ingots and coins, that was supposedly stored in a strong room below the *Loanda's* bridge, was ever found is not known. Nonetheless, every time a diver visits the wreck the thought of all that hidden silver must be foremost on his or her mind.

The Flores remaining anchor came fast on the Malms Rocks

PIER PRESSURE

The 'fore and aft' schooner *Flores* limped into the Downs on Friday, January 6th 1911. The Brazilian craft had set sail from Hamburg, with a general cargo and a German crew, bound for her home port of Maceio. The *Flores* had a broken main boom and this was the reason why her long journey to that Atlantic port had been diverted.

Within the hour a Deal galley had hooked on and moored up alongside the little 47 ton schooner. The master of the *Flores*, Captain Fickel, had conversed with the local skipper and made him aware of his predicament. A price was agreed for the galley's charter and a shipwright was brought out to measure up for the replacement spar. By Monday, the work had been done and the wooden boom had been ferried out and transferred aboard. After the bill had been settled, the skipper of the galley wished the captain goodbye and a pleasant voyage – however, he warned the master that he felt there was a storm brewing.

The weather was bitter and the wind had freshened. The German seamen felt cold and their fingers were numb as they re-rigged the sail to the new boom. Fickel knew it was going to be a long and arduous voyage in their small craft and, after some thought, he decided to wait for the weather to moderate.

By Wednesday the barometer had started to drop. The sudden fall of mercury was recorded to almost an inch. In the early hours of Thursday morning, 12th January, the strong south-west breeze dropped to calm. Then half an hour later, through the blackness, there was an enormous sound of wind – at three o'clock, the north-north-east gale struck.

At daybreak, all the ships that were lying in the Downs were straining at their anchors. Tugs had arrived from Dover and were engaged in assisting the vessels that were damaged — or in imminent danger of collision through dragging their anchors. The tugs were being kept very busy as the gale continued to rage. Getting a tow aboard a casualty in the heavy sea conditions was exceedingly difficult.

The *Flores* had both anchors down, with the maximum amount of chain cable streaming out through her hawse-holes. With the force of the wind increasing the ebb tide, the little vessel slowly dragged towards Deal pier. Shortly before 10 o'clock her rigging caught onto the gas lamps on the south-east corner of the cast iron structure and in a shower of glass, ripped them off.

Her anchors were coming home (dragging over the ground) and she increased her drift ever closer to the shore. The Dover Harbour tug, *Lady Vita*, made a desperate dash to render assistance, however she could not get close enough to the rolling vessel to help. The *Flores'* only chance of salvation would have been to sail away from the lee shore.

A small amount of canvas was set and then the crew of the *Flores* struggled to heave her anchors aboard. They successfully hauled aboard one, but when the next was half way in, the cable jammed in the windlass.

The roll of the small craft was becoming even more violent in the shallow water. Her crew were having difficulty standing, let alone trying to work on deck. Surf was crashing against the sides of the vessel, drenching the men.

Suddenly, the rolling motion ceased. The schooner started to pitch, and her head swung around to face the seas – the anchor had come fast in the rock bank that was adjacent to Deal Castle. Now, at times, she buried her bow into the next wave. The Malms Rocks had given the *Flores* brief salvation.

While this was going on, the beach had become crowded with onlookers. With the schooner being so close to shore, the people could see every movement that her crew made. The local coastguards had also turned-up, bringing with them their Board of Trade rocket apparatus.

The crew on the *Flores* decided that they had had enough. Every one of them was exhausted – they had been struggling against the elements for too long. As they were powerless to do any more they wearily put on their life-belts. With the bedraggled ship's cat cradled in one of their arms they stood, braced against the pitch of the schooner, waiting to be rescued.

Walmer lifeboat was already on standby. Her coxswain could see all that was going on as the *Flores* was only a couple of hundred yards north from their station. Their problem would be the wind direction – it was head-on to the lifeboat. Nevertheless, they decided to have a go.

The launch was mistimed. Gracefully the lifeboat slid down the greased woods, but the craft found a receding wave and promptly buried her keel into the shingle beach. The next three mountainous waves hit her bow and slewed her around almost broadside on to the incoming sea. Amongst the cascading surf, the lifeboat crew pulled on their haul-off rope, that was attached out to sea by a large anchor. Slowly the lifeboat made it off the beach and the men set her sail to clear the surf.

A crewman being rescued by breeches buoy

Awaiting just off-shore was the tug, *Lady Vita*. However, perhaps due to the shallow water, she did not make any attempt to assist the lifeboat.

It was left up to the lifeboat coxswain and his crew to make the difficult tacks into the wind and try to reach the *Flores*. Their task looked impossible, nevertheless they kept trying.

Hundreds of people were on the beach and surrounded the coastguards as they set up their rocket launching equipment. They were all trying to help, but only succeeded in getting in the way. Although the coastguards had had regular practice with the rocket gear, this was to be the first time it had been used in a service for 15 years.

With a loud report, the rocket was fired towards the *Flores* and a cloud of smoke engulfed the crowd. Their aim was perfect and the missile landed over the schooner, just forward of her foremast. The ropes were hauled on-board.

Soon after they were made fast the first two men were dragged to safety in the breeches buoy. The harness was quickly drawn back to the stricken vessel by the over-enthusiastic crowd. They were becoming a danger to the rescue and the coastguards were having a job controlling them.

Just as the third man was hauled ashore the anchor chain of the *Flores* snapped. The vessel, that minutes before had her head to the sea and wind, was now at its mercy.

The wind whipped the schooner's bow a full 180 degrees to the south. The craft wrapped the shoreline around her masts, pulling it free from the moorings ashore. Rope and pebbles flew across the beach, scattering all in its way. *Flores* now released from her tether came crashing ashore in an avalanche of dirty grey water.

She shuddered with every sea that hit her and waves swept over her deck. Captain Fickel appeared calm, however, his remaining crewman was distraught. He made an attempt to abandon the rolling vessel and jump into the boiling surf. His captain made no move to stop him – oddly he seemed mesmerised and resigned to his fate.

George Baker, a local boatman, rushed forward, shouting to the man not to move. He ran into the water and threw a rope on to the *Flores* and the man secured it to the mast. When that was done the remaining crewmember slid down it on to the beach. The captain of the *Flores* made no attempt to follow. Baker shinned up the rope and spoke to Fickel. After a while he managed to convince him to abandon his vessel. As the captain reached the shingle a loud cheer arose from the crowd.

With the departure of the skipper, more Deal boatmen scrambled aboard the derelict vessel. They made her fast to a nearby capstan, untangled the coastguard's tackle, furled the sails and cleared the cordage. When the tide receded the *Flores* was left high and dry.

The boatmen hoped that they could refloat her, however on the next day Mr. Cullen, a shipbuilder from Dover, declared the schooner to be a total wreck. As soon as this was known the longshoremen stripped her of the cargo and gear. The ship's cat was found cowering in the forepeak and was taken by the local vet to be put into quarantine. By 10 o'clock that night there was nothing left of value upon her. On the Sunday, her masts were cut away and the hulk was left for fire-wood.

Mr Prior, the agent for shipwrecked mariners, cared for the captain and crew of the *Flores*. He took them to the local Wesleyan church where they attended the service. They prayed for thanks at being saved – and one of the crew admitted that this was the second time that he had been rescued from the clutches of a shipwreck in the Downs.

Deal boatmen strip the *Flores* of anything of value

Aries was an elegant steam yacht owned by the Duke of Leeds

MINEFIELD

The second day of November 1915, the Admiralty completed a Court of Enquiry into the loss of His Majesty's Yacht, *Aries*, which was sunk on the 31st October, of that same year.

The clerk of the court neatly typed up 23 pages of the evidence. Throughout those pages were recorded the answers from the officers who had witnessed the sinking of not only the *Aries* but also the armed trawler, *Othello II,* and the steamships *Toward* and *Eidvisa*. A total of 2,784 tons of shipping had been lost in a couple of hours. Most of the questions were answered with a short 'Yes Sir' or 'No Sir'. Occasionally the eyewitnesses were asked to elaborate, however, even then this did not warrant much more than a couple of sentences.

It was noted that one of the officers – a survivor of the *Aries* – was given some allowances if his statements were disjointed. The reason being that, although uninjured, he was evidently suffering considerably from shock as the result of his experience.

At the end of the report it was concluded that... 'With regard to the loss of HMY *Aries* we are of the opinion that she sank as a result of striking an enemy mine. We regret in our opinion her Commanding Officer committed an error in proceeding for the purpose of endeavouring to locate and sink a mine, into an area which was under suspicion of being mined and which had been closed to traffic for some days, more especially as two steamers had been sunk in close proximity only an hour or two before.' However, in ink, on the front of the report, a note was written by the Vice-Admiral of the Dover Patrol' *...'No disciplinary action is possible against the Commanding Officer of Aries, as he has unfortunately lost his life. Otherwise concur.* Their 'Lordships' had spoken.

The incident happened along with the heavy weather which normally occurs in the latter part of October. A severe gale had arisen from the south-south-east and was reluctant to abate. This had caused a disruption to the Admiralty minesweepers. The route, between the Goodwin Sands and Dover that the merchant ships passed through, could not be checked for mines. The wait of a day or two was unacceptable to the civilian captains and they complained bitterly to the Commander-in-Chief of the Dover Patrol. Nevertheless, for the last 48 hours it had been too rough for the trawler minesweepers to be at sea and there was nothing further that could be done.

In the early hours of 30th October 1915, there seemed to be a slight moderation in the gale. The shipping channel, 'A' route, was going to be swept by the armed trawlers *Jackmar* and *Othello II*. Unfortunately the *Jackmar* had difficulties with her kite (a fitting which keeps the wire that the minesweeper is towing at a certain depth) and had to return to harbour.

The 'A' route had been clear of mines for up to 14 days previously, however, what the Admiralty did not realise was that the night before a German submarine had entered the channel and laid its deadly cargo of mines.

Mattias Graf von Schmettow in command of the *UC-6* of the Flanders Flotilla, had sneaked in under the cover of the bad weather. He jettisoned, from the tubes of the mine laying submarine, half of his load of 14 mines. Schmettow took his time. Normally this part of the coast would have been swarming with British Naval vessels, all on the look-out for U boats or enemy raiders. Once he had finished laying the mines, he took his craft out of the shipping lane, looking for pastures new.

The first ship to hit his mines was the Norwegian steamship, *Eidvisa*. Minutes later the Clyde Shipping Company's vessel, *Toward*, ploughed into another one – a few hundred yards away from her predecessor. It was never decided who had given the order to allow the impatient merchantmen to resume their voyage through the Dover Straits before the route had been cleared, but they were paying the price now.

The gale was still blowing as the *Aries* approached the devastation area from the South Goodwins. She was escorting three divisions of drifters which had been on duty that night. They had been out in mid-Channel tending the anti-submarine nets and were looking forward to some relief.

Aries was an elegant steam yacht owned by the Duke of Leeds. He had graciously lent it to the Admiralty for war service. Although all of her luxurious leather chairs had been put in storage; she still kept her ornate brass fittings that showed the decadence of the aristocracy. Built in 1881 at Barrow, she was an excellent seagoing vessel. There had been hardly any alterations made to her by the admiralty except the inclusion of a three pounder fore and aft.

Lieutenant Commander Calder RNR was proud to be the skipper of such a fine craft. His crew were often ribbed ashore, as being the men off the 'posh ship'. Nevertheless their accommodation, compared with that of the drifters and trawlers, more than made up for all the sarcasm. As the *Aries* was in command of the drifter divisions, she also had the benefit of a wireless and operator.

Calder, by the aid of semaphore, ordered the trawlers, who had picked up the survivors from the merchantmen, to be taken back to Dover. Flags from another trawler reported other sightings of a floating mine and the armed yacht went to investigate.

At that time, the bridge of the *Aries* was full of the ships officers. The captain requested that Sub-lieutenant Cranfield should go forward to look for the mine – it was an order that was to save Cranfield's life.

The Sub-lieutenant knew he was in full view of the bridge and therefore said few words to the two forward gunners who were at attendance to their weapon. As he looked seaward, he did not see the mine that struck the armed yacht amidships.

With an ear-deafening explosion, the ship broke in half. The engineers would not have known a thing as the mine totally annihilated the engine room. The captain and most of the officers on the bridge were ripped to shreds with the torn, flying metal which had been previously beneath their feet. As the upward thrust of the explosion demolished the bridge their broken and shattered thigh bones protruded, and blood splattered over the polished brass fittings. In an instant, the two halves of the ship began to sink.

Through the smoke and debris, Cranfield could hardly believe his eyes. The once proud vessel was disappearing into the dirty, gale swept sea. He briefly saw a lieutenant and the assistant paymaster struggling up to their knees in water. Before he could call out to them, they vanished from sight.

In a flurry of escaping air and steam the *Aries* sank in 15 fathoms, less than a mile off the South Foreland lighthouse. In the water with Cranfield were the two forward gunners. Fortunately both men were uninjured apart from traumatic shock. They said nothing and, along with the sub-lieutenant, they fought to stay afloat in the cold, rough sea.

Amongst the floating debris, a hundred feet away, was the wireless operator who had a badly bleeding head wound and broken ribs. Keeping him company was an AB from the stern gun, also with broken ribs.

Being at the extreme ends of the ship, and furthest away from the explosion, was the only explanation for the survival of these men.

Out of the *Aries* crew of 28 only those five were found alive.

Rescue came quickly in the form of another trawler. As the floundering men were helped aboard, another detonation was heard over the shriek of the gale. This time it was the mine sweeper *Othello II* which fell foul of the *UC-6's* deadly mines.

The trawler sank immediately; the sole survivor from her crew was the ship's boy. He had been pushed through the window of the wheel-house when the explosion had jammed the door shut. In hindsight, if her companion trawler the *Jackmar* had not had difficulties with her gear, they would have swept the area and would have discovered the minefield.

Although the captain of the *Aries* was posthumously blamed for her loss, the courage of these men must be admired. Following orders to the exact letter was difficult for these sailors when trying to save lives and ships. Under the hard conditions they excelled themselves and much was owed to their bravery. However, the Admiralty had to do every thing by the book – although that did not stop them from secretly approving of their deeds.

The Admiralty informed George Godolphin, the tenth Duke of Leeds, of the loss of his beloved yacht. As he had lent her to the navy, perhaps it was down to him to finance the replacement of his vessel.

The wreck of the *Aries* is very much a war grave, which lies beneath the sea. She is fittingly overlooked by the Dover Patrol Memorial obelisk, high above, on the white cliffs.

Nonetheless, another armed yacht, the *Marcella*, which lies to the north of her went down with no loss of life. She had been involved in a collision in 1916. This wreck site has been, and still is, a favourite divers' haunt.

Hierarchy of the Dover Patrol

John Maxted and Gerry Dowd with the recovered *Etoile Polaire's* bell

NARROW ESCAPE

Apart from wages, the only other legal way of making money in the Royal Navy was from taking a prize, sinking a U-boat or salvage. Either way, sailors had to rely on the whims of the Admiralty on the amount that was paid out.

The 278 ton *Etoile Polaire* was not, as would be expected with that name, a French vessel. She was a brand new, British deep-sea trawler that the Admiralty had hired as soon as she was built in March, 1915. The trawlers had already proven themselves as work-horses and she was gratefully received into the Dover Patrol to relieve their work load.

One of her first jobs was to escort a cable ship out to the *Sunk* light vessel off the Essex coast. A break in the lightship's telephone wire had caused problems with communication ashore and, whilst they waited for the cable ship to render the repair, a loud explosion occurred. Near-by, they saw the merchant vessel, *Volician,* had hit a mine and was sinking. In a panic, the ship's crew had abandoned their vessel before the *Etoile Polaire* could get alongside. Seconds after the *Volicain's* lifeboat had made fast to the trawler's side the seamen were clambering aboard in a condition of terror. The armed trawler's crew were sympathetic; the mine had been the fear of sailors since the beginning of the war – it was never known where and when it would strike.

The *Etoile Polaire's* skipper saw that, although the steamer was down by her head, she had not settled further in the water. He inquired with the *Volician's* captain and crew if they would like to re-board their ship. There was no hesitation in their reply and he was told, in no uncertain terms, 'no'. Nevertheless, he felt sure there was a chance of saving the vessel. Without hesitation, volunteers from his own men went aboard and secured a tow.

Slowly they pulled the steamship against a strong tide and through the dangerous sandbanks and British mine fields. Eventually they made their way to the *Rough* buoy off

Harwich. It was there, close to the port, that two tugs came out and relieved them of their heavy tow.

The ss *Volician's* value was reported to be £10,000, however, the *Etoile Polaire's* master and crew only received an award of £75 – to be shared between them. British sailors have always had contempt for the hierarchy in the Admiralty and this incident added fuel to the fire. Even the Commander-in-Chief of the Dover Patrol, Vice Admiral Bacon, was astounded at their miserly payment.

After this incident, the Dover Patrol kept the trawler and her crew busier closer to home. With a gun mounted forward of her wheelhouse she was used for escort as well as anti-submarine work.

On the night of 3rd December 1915, her short career with the navy was going to be abruptly terminated.

Close to the south part of the Goodwins, it was a deadly mine that exploded on contact with the *Etoile Polaire's* hull and ripped her bows apart. Smoke and steam emitted from below deck as water entered her boiler room. The crew's deafened ears did not hear the vessel's death groans as the bulkheads gave way under the weight of sea flowing into the gaping hole in her bow. As if in a daze, the skipper and crew had hardly time to get into the small ship's boat before she sank beneath them. Only nine months old, this trawler had died before the smell of fish had ever entered her holds.

The sea was rough with a fresh south-west wind and the tide was flooding to the north-north-east, which swept the boat and men towards the Goodwin Sands.

In the darkness the men huddled on the boat's thwarts. All around them were the tumultuous waves – which were threatening to swamp their rowing boat at any time. They knew that if they capsized they would not survive long in those freezing cold conditions.

With his men on the oars, the trawler's skipper headed the row-boat into the waves, on a south-west course. Although they had no visual way-point to aim for, he realised it would be in the general direction of Dover.

The wind and tide were stronger than their efforts and they soon heard the continuous beating sound of the surf pounding on to the Goodwin Sands. Fortunately the tide started to ease, nevertheless they still kept up their frantic strokes on the oars. The rowers' eyes widened on their spray-drenched faces when they could see, breaking on the sandbank, the towering waves that whipped the sea into foam-flecked nightmares of confused violence. Suddenly, they realised that they were making headway, away from the danger. The tide had changed.

Now the seas grew larger as the wind scoured against the tide. The men on the oars were only just managing to keep the boat's head into the sea. As the tide picked up, the *Etoile Polaire's* skipper knew that he would be swept past the port of Dover. He realised that they had only just managed to save themselves from the clutches of the Goodwins – now their fate would be to die from exposure or drown. The men were growing tired and the coldness was starting to numb their bodies.

Suddenly, out of the darkness, they saw the dim riding-light of an anchored ship. The skipper immediately recognized it as the *South Goodwin* light vessel; however, it was several hundred yards off their port bow. The men knew their only chance of salvation would be to reach the lightship – before the tide could sweep them past. They pulled on their oars with a will. Now the seas were breaking dangerously on and into the small rowing boat. The men who were not rowing, were bailing out manically. Desperation and fatigue overcame caution. The clinker-planked boat was filling with water, yet they still rowed with urgency.

They only just reached the *South Goodwin* and their rowing boat scraped down the hull's side with the tide. The men became anxious as their hands failed to find anything to grasp on to. Their cries for help thankfully alerted the lightship crewman who had been on watch and, on seeing their plight, he quickly threw a rope down to them.

It was almost pulled out of their clutching hands. Every one of them was exhausted; they had been fighting the sea and wind too long. With the waves, wind and tide, the small boat crashed against the *South Goodwin's* hull. With haste, they made the boat fast and clambered up the Jacob's ladder that had been lowered. The rowing boat, which had been their deliverance, succumbed to the battering and sank.

It was fortunate that the crew of the *Etoile Polaire* had seen the lightship. The *South Goodwin* had not been displaying her normal two flashes every 30 seconds. War had subdued her brilliance. In the past the enemy had used the light as a navigational position for their occasional, but audacious, night raids. The Admiralty had decided it was an advantage *they* could do without. Providentially for the rescued men, the vessel was still manned and had a wireless link to the shore.

The lightship-men tended to the *Etoile Polaire's* sea-drenched crew; warm blankets were wrapped around them and they were given hot drinks. The lieutenant in command of the sunken trawler declared his thanks and reported the loss of his trawler. By wireless his plight was relayed ashore and, shortly after, they were picked up and taken back to Dover. They were the lucky ones – usually the loss of an Admiralty trawler by a mine strike meant death or maiming.

The Ministry of Defence Hydrographic Office (Wrecks Section) at Taunton in Somerset records all new and old wrecks that have occurred. They do their best to put names to the inert lumps of metal and wood that litter the seabed, however, they rely on divers to enlighten them on any mistakes. One such mistake was a wreck, positioned close to the Goodwin Sands, that the Hydrogrphic Office had named the *U-16*.

Half-way through the dive season of 2002, Gerry Dowd in his boat *Excel 3*, found a completely contradictory site than that of a U-boat. On his first dive, he discovered an upright wreck with a rounded stern, facing north. To the south, the bow was entirely mangled. A gun, with the barrel pointing down at an angle of 45 degrees, was found close to the wreck's bridge – it had fallen through the rotting deck. Aft of the wheelhouse, in the crew's accommodation, he found .303 rifle cartridges

Part of the *Etoile Polaire* still survives

scattered amongst broken crockery and bottles. Although the engine and boilers were almost covered with sand, the stern of the vessel was completely intact. Gerry found a brass Walker's log that was still in its bracket, fixed to the transom by the stern rail. The conclusion was that this was obviously not a U-boat.

Gerry had dived on wrecks like this before around the Goodwins and he instantly recognised the wreck to be an armed trawler. As he swam around the rusting hulk, a dull glimmer of non-ferrous metal caught his eye – it was the ship's bell. Rubbing the green verdigris from the bell the letters **ETOILE POLAIRE** could clearly be seen. After 87 years the correct resting place for this trawler could now be charted.

The Admiralty made the trawlers the 'Jack-of-all-trades'

LOST PATROL

It is a little known fact that there are at least twenty Hull and Grimsby deep sea fishing vessels sunk within eyesight of the Goodwin Sands. It has not been the fish stocks that have attracted these vessels to their doom, but two World Wars. Artic and North Sea trawlers were an ideal 'Jack-of-all-trades' craft for the Royal Navy and the majority were easily converted into mine-sweepers and anti-submarine vessels. These gallant little ships made up the mainstay of the Dover Patrol. Throughout the First World War, it was estimated that the trawlers had swept the equivalent of 12 times around the earth, just to keep the Dover Straits shipping lanes relatively clear of mines.

The total complement to crew a trawler would be at least 10 hands, which ranged from the skipper to the decky learner – although now that they had become navy personnel they were ranked lieutenant to ordinary seaman. Most of these men were ex-fishermen whose calling had been disrupted by the war. Nevertheless, these brave sailors were patriotic enough to volunteer as soon as they were needed.

They were a rough and ready lot with characters to match and the streets of Dover reverberated on many a Saturday night to their northern accents. Slowly but surely they realised the dangers of war and conformed to orders and discipline. Their increasing duties gave them less time for 'the beer' and they always worked with a will. They became fearless and did not question their tasks which, at times, were hard and dirty. It was their courage that helped Britain win the war.

Although they were used to the rough waters of the Arctic and North Sea, the crews of the trawlers and drifters were soon to witness the severity of a gale in these narrow seas. In the early hours of the 4th February 1916, a whole gale raged from the south-south-west and the sea in the Channel was extremely heavy.

Most of that night, the noise of the gale had kept many of the Deal populace from their sleep. North Deal lifeboat coxswain, William Adams, was up early. Before first light, he walked along to the lifeboat house to check on the conditions of the beach. If the seas had piled the shingle up too high in front of the lifeboat station, he knew that the *Charles Dibden* could not launch. It would take time and men with shovels, to clear a course-way through the pebbles.

It was half past five in the morning and he strained his eyes through the darkness searching for the loom of dawn. As he looked seaward, he spied flares being fired at the back of the Goodwins Sands. He rushed to awaken his crew and, in their state of tiredness, they prepared the lifeboat for a launch.

Being low tide, and so early in the morning, the small amount of shore helpers who had turned out were hard-stretched to place the greased woods in front of the lifeboat. These woods were to enable the craft to slide down the shingle beach and into the sea. When the *Charles Dibden* was let go, she came to an abrupt halt before the vessel could get afloat. The low water mark had exposed flat sand on what was normally a sloping shingle beach.

Extreme shallow water was a peculiarity that North Deal did not share with Walmer and Kingsdown, situated a few miles to the south.

The *Charles Dibden,* weighing 10½ tons, was eventually manhandled into the sea. Even then she did not have enough water under her keel to float her off. Restlessly they waited for the tide to make, and at seven o'clock on that wind-blown morning, with great difficulty, they sailed the lifeboat through the surf.

On reaching the eastward side of the Goodwins they found the Admiralty trawler, *De La Pole*, aground on the Sands. She was in a sorry state — mountainous seas were breaking over the half submerged hull and the crew were hanging on to both the pulpit rails on the foredeck and the rigging of the foremast. The trawler's skipper stood defiantly on the fore-bridge of the partially submerged wheelhouse, up to his thighs in water. With the making tide, the vessel was slowly disappearing before the lifeboat men's eyes.

As spray sleeted across William Adams face he blinked and barely noticed it. Swiftness would be essential to save these men but he knew mistakes could cost lives – even their own. He steered the lifeboat up-wind and let go the heavy anchor. As he dropped astern towards the strickened trawler, the waves were getting larger. When one buried the vessel in a cascade of dirty green sea a man was torn from the wire forestay of the wreck. He crashed into the maelstrom below and the crew of the *Charles Dibden* were powerless to save him. Although ropes were cast in his direction the man was too weak to assist in saving his own life. He was quickly swept away and out of sight.

Lines were thrown to the rest of the men on the bow of the *De La Pole*. Not one of them could – or would – release their hand-hold to catch it. The lifeboat's bowman let out more anchor rope, allowing the craft to close in on the wreck. The conditions were getting horrendous and the surf reared and roared around the grounded trawler. In these circumstances Adams was finding it difficult to prevent the *Charles Dibden* from pounding into the wave-battered hulk. A heaving-line attached to a grapnel fortunately managed to get caught on to the rails on the *De La Pole's* foredeck and they pulled the lifeboat close enough to get the first man off.

The survivors were near death. They had been clinging on for hours in the freezing elements and they were incapable of helping themselves. Each and every man had to be pulled off and be helped by the willing lifeboat men. Once onboard, they lay motionless in the bottom of the boat. The coxswain ordered a small quantity rum to be administered, but it did little to revive the men.

The captain of the trawler was still clinging to the bridge rails with the water now above his waist. William Adams was at a loss as to what to do. He could not get any closer to the wreck or they all would perish. *De La Pole's* skipper realised this and took the situation out of the old lifeboat man's hands when he jumped into the foaming sea. Fortunately the tide carried him to within 30 feet of the *Charles Dibden*. A cane-line* was hastily cast towards the captain.

However, in those conditions the projectile missed. Quickly it was pulled back and the line promptly flaked down on the deck. With a carefully calculated throw, the cane fell over the struggling man's shoulder and, with what little energy he had left, the valiant captain clutched hold of it.

This time the sea did not win.

When the poor man was hauled over the gunnels of the boat, the crew thought he had expired – he lay there unmoving.

These Deal boatmen who manned the lifeboat had no training in medicine, but they cared for the rescued trawler's crew the best they could. Along with the captain, four other men were in a state of near unconsciousness. Adams's meagre supply of rum and water would not be enough to revive these wet and cold men and he knew that he had to get them safely ashore before they died.

To save time, Adams ordered the anchor cable to be cut and 40 fathoms of rope was abandoned. They hoisted the main and mizzen sail and cleared the wreck. The *Charles Dibden,* released from her bondage, rode the crests of the waves freely. The coxswain had trepidations about the route home that he had to take – through the gap in the Sands called Kellet Gut. Normally this part of the Sands was navigated with the visual signs of the calmer water indicating the deeper channel. This time waves poured in long confused masses towards the lifeboat and broke all around them. He reefed in the sails, yet that did not slow the boat down as she bumped through the swatch-way.

Some relief was gained as they cleared the Goodwins and came into slightly deeper water. The *Charles Dibden* still pitched and rolled in the rough seas, nevertheless, her crew continued to support and comfort the injured men. The flood tide was running hard to the north – the southerly gale had increased the run by an extra knot or two. Adams knew it would take an age to beat back towards the beach and it could be the time his rescued men did not have.

The motion of the lifeboat steadied as she changed course and sailed with the wind and tide. Her sails pulled tight as she headed towards Broadstairs. The old lifeboat coxswain had decided this was going to be their quickest haven of safety to reach. It was usual for the Deal boats to sail there when the weather was too adverse for beaching and doing so this time would save the lives of the *De la Pole's* sailors.

William Adams received a silver medal from the Royal National Lifeboat Institution for this save; however, he always acknowledged that it could not have been successfully performed without his gallant crew.

The wreck lay undiscovered and uncharted for 81 years until it was uncovered and was explored by the divers from Allan Booth's Ramsgate charter boat *Bonaventure II*. They found the trawler still intact and with her funnel in situ. They also noted that her stern looked as if it had been rammed. It was never recorded why the *De La Pole* ended up on the Goodwins. Perhaps a mine had disabled her or even a collision, or maybe it was just the power of the seas beating on the Goodwin Sands…

* This was a weighted stick which was attached to a safety line and could normally be thrown with great accuracy.

Close to the *Gull* lightship was the resting place of the *Piave*

MAIDEN VOYAGE

In the nineteenth and early part of the twentieth-century, the lightships had the means of making a signal to the shore if they saw a ship in distress. They would have a code which would avoid confusion and be clearly understood by the lifeboat coxswain ashore. If the *Gull* light vessel saw a shipwreck on the northern portion of the Goodwin Sands, one gun would be fired every three minutes. On the middle part of the Sands, a wreck would warrant the first gun fired, then thirty seconds later a second one, this double signal being repeated every five minutes. For a vessel on the south part of the Goodwins one gun fired every five minutes; and if a ship was upon the north-west Sands, or the Brake sandbank, the signal would be two guns at fifteen seconds interval, repeated every five minutes. At night, rockets would accompany the guns.

Two days before the end of a very cold January 1919, the *Gull* light vessel's cannons fired off her code along with a pyrotechnic display. Through the darkness there was hardly any need to advertise the position of the ship in distress. The 6,869 ton American ship *Piave* was aground close to the lightship with every light that she possessed switched on – which lit the ship up like a Christmas tree.

This had been the *Piave's* maiden voyage from New York. She had her holds filled with much wanted food for war torn Europe. Her cargo was to be landed at their next port of call, Rotterdam. However, without a pilot, the ship had managed to run up onto the Goodwins with a rising tide.

At ten-thirty that night, William Adams launched the Deal lifeboat *Charles Dibden*. The wind was coming dead on shore from the east and, through the occasional snow flurry, he had to sail on a long tack northward towards Sandwich Bay. He then changed course and beat to windward and reached the *Piave* an hour-and-a-half later. In the wintry weather, his crew felt frozen. Three of them with numbed limbs had difficulty in climbing the ladder that had been offered to them from the side of the *Piave's* towering hull.

The lifeboat's crewmen were dazzled by the ship's deck lights, nevertheless, they inquired as to whereabouts of the ship's captain. They were astonished, but accepted the courteous reply, that he was sound asleep. Furthermore, they were informed that he was not to be awakened before seven-thirty the following morning.

Along with the lifeboat, three Dover tugs, *Lady Crundell*, *Lady Duncannon* and *Lady Brasey*, had turned up. These vessels stood-by just out of the reach of the shallow water. They hailed the lifeboat and the salvage master was transferred on to her. He requested Adams to put him alongside the *Piave*.

Captain John Iron was not only Dover's harbour master but also the Admiralty's chief salvage officer. He was a third generation descendant of Dover's harbour masters and had learnt his trade from his father and grandfather. He was a no-nonsense man and there were few who could equal him in his expertise.

Once aboard the *Piave*, Iron demanded that the ship's captain should be immediately awakened. Shortly after, the sleepy captain appeared. He was an elderly Norwegian, who previously had been a farmer in America some years before the war. Iron did his best to convince the captain of the seriousness of the situation and the urgency to get his ship off the deadly sandbank. The Norwegian reluctantly agreed and retired back to his cabin. Throughout the early hours the tugs' hawsers were attached and, at six-thirty on the morning of the 30th January, the first attempt to pull her off failed.

The *Charles Dibden*, which was tied up alongside the steamship, only carried an emergency ration of a few biscuits, a jar of water and a small amount of rum. Some of the *Piave's* crew had made the lifeboat men welcome and as comfortable as they could. Aboard the *Piave*, they were supplied with hot food and drink which was eaten in the comfort of this new ship's dinning room. It would be a comfort that they were to deserve as the lifeboat would be in attendance for many hours.

After the first attempt to tow the ship off had failed, William Adams's crewmen willingly assisted the Americans to lighten their vessel. Overboard went sacks of flour, sides of bacon and vast slabs of lard. Soon after, three more tugs arrived and with six of them now trying to pull the *Piave* off they still could not budge her. The icy wind had freshened and swung slightly to the south and the snow squalls made their life a misery.

Although the salvage was still going ahead, the old lifeboat coxswain knew that there could be a chance that the vessel would be another Goodwin Sands victim. The *Piave* was straddled across the tide and the sand was building up amidships, leaving the bow and stern clear. He confided with the Norwegian captain that if he and his crew should have to abandon their ship he would transfer them to safety. On no account should they attempt to launch their own lifeboats.

1,500 tons of fuel oil was next to be pumped out. The sea gulls that had been attracted to the ship's jettisoned food cargo were soon smothered in the foul smelling liquid. They struggled to get clear but soon died. The oil would kill hundreds of sea birds and pollute the beaches of Deal and Dover for a long while after. Regardless of all these efforts the ship had stubbornly failed to move an inch.

On the third day, at two in the afternoon, Captain Iron felt the ship quivering. He warned everyone that she was going to break in half. Whilst Iron was removing his salvage gear, the captain of the *Piave* entrusted him with not only the ship's papers but also £30,000. Two hours later the wind had risen to a strong blow and the sea-spray was being highlighted in the glare of the Piave's deck lights.

With a noise not unlike rifle shots, the rivets on the hull in the engine room started to fly off. By four-thirty, the safety valve on the boiler burst. Next to break was the main propeller shaft. Within the following hour, the ship broke in half and all of the lights were extinguished.

Above and below decks pandemonium erupted. The crew of 96 men panicked in the darkness and were rushing around trying to seek salvation. Men jumped off the side of the hull as half of the massive ship fell over 25 degrees to port. William Adams, in the *Charles Dibden*, knew his time for action had come.

When Adams heard the command to lower one of the *Piave's* lifeboats, he could not believe his ears. As soon as they made her ready 20 men scrambled aboard. When lowering the lifeboat the after tackle gave way and, with a jerk, the craft hung in the falls by her bow. All of the 20 men were thrown into the rough, cold sea.

Chaos abounded – all around the weather side of the ship seamen were floundering in the water. Each and every one of the crew in the lifeboat was busy with rescuing men and, in the confusion, there was a danger of people being crushed between the ship and the lifeboat. Another threat was that the tide would carry them away in the night and be lost from sight. One man was only saved when, in the darkness, the lifeboat's battery powered search-light reflected off the top of his white cap. Through the turmoil, Adams called to those aboard the *Piave* to jump into the *Charles Dibden* as he sheered the lifeboat against the hull. He watched in astonished disbelief when another two full lifeboats were launched.

Fortunately the Ramsgate lifeboat had arrived and between them they saved the *Piave's* crew. The Deal boat cautiously towed the overcrowded ship's lifeboat through the rough sea to the waiting tugs. The tugs were standing away from the wreck and outside of the broken water on the Goodwin Sands.

The ordeal of the *Charles Dibden* was not yet over. On the Goodwins there is occasionally a tidal phenomenon which causes a maelstrom. The lifeboat was caught and became out of control in a whirlpool which spun her around almost fifty times. It took a cresting wave to break her free from its grips. With 29 of the *Piave's* crew onboard, the *Charles Dibden* sailed for home. She was closely followed by the Ramsgate lifeboat with 23 rescued men – the remainder of the steamship's crew were taken back to Dover on the tugs. Eventually the Deal lifeboat reached the shore – their trial afloat had lasted 50 hours.

Within seven days the two halves of the *Piave* had sunk into the Sands and the masts were barely showing above the sea at high tide. The sand on that part of the bank must have been at its deepest as the ship was totally swallowed up and has disappeared without a trace.

Lifeboat crew pulling on the haul-off rope to launch the *Charles Dibden*

27

SANDS OF DEATH

Death affects everybody in different ways. Sadness consumes the mind along with loss. Nevertheless, when death could have been avoided, the mind is not only filled with melancholy but also frustration and bitterness. Such were the feelings of the Deal lifeboat coxswain and his crew on the night of November 1st, 1919.

As the *North Goodwin*, *East Goodwin* and *Gull* lightships started to fire their guns and rockets, preparations were going ahead to launch the Deal lifeboat, *Charles Dibden*. An east-north-east gale had been raging from the day before and the seas were endlessly pounding upon the beach. At a quarter to 11 in the evening, the lifeboat was let go from her slip chain and she sped down the shingle beach. The incoming waves halted her momentum for a mere second at the same time as the crew hoisted her sails. The coxswain, William Adams, dropped the rudder home and the base of the iron pintles crashed against the gudgeons that were attached to the stern post. Slowly and laboriously, the *Charles Dibden* clawed her way against the gale and towards the Goodwins Sands.

With all three lightships firing signals, coxswain Adams decided to head for the closest one first, to ascertain where the casualty was. After three hours of beating against the wind, he gradually closed in on the *Gull* light vessel. Before they reached the ship, his crew alerted him that they could see a schooner, awash on the starboard beam. With seas breaking over the bow, the drenched men manoeuvred the lifeboat up-tide to the wreck. With the wind on their port quarter, the coxswain ordered the kedge anchor to be let go.

Before they could haul down their mainsail and veer out the anchor cable, a large steamer appeared on their bow — heading directly at them!

Will Adams could not believe his eyes. The ship, being empty of cargo and high in the water, looked enormous. Adams's reason raced ahead, trying to solve the situation that he and his crew were in. They were being tossed about in the confused sea, that the flood tide was creating against the wind; nevertheless, the lifeboat was now in a position to make the save. Was he to let out the cable and ignore the ship, which was still approaching on a collision course, or get out of her way? He ordered some of the crew to ignite flares, to signal and thus attract the attention of the steamer to their predicament. The rest of the crew

The lifeboat battles against the elements

were shouting as loud as they could, however the roar of the gale reduced their voices to mere whispers.

In the flare's incandescence the apprehensive crews' faces glowed as they looked first towards the approaching menace and then at the shipwreck. From the light, they could see six pitiful survivors clinging to the schooner's rigging and two more holding on to another part of the wreck.

At the last moment the lifeboat coxswain took avoiding action. He shouted curses as the ship narrowly missed them and continued on her way. He almost expected, and secretly hoped, that she would strike the Sands at any moment. The unidentified ship, being light in the water, survived that ordeal.

Again, with difficulty, Adams positioned the *Charles Dibden* up tide from the wreck. With the anchor down, they let the lifeboats main cable slowly inch its way out from around the sampson

William Adams

post. The coxswain positioned the rudder, sheering the little craft closer to the casualty.

Adams was calm now – and he and his crew were working as a team. Although the unnecessary delay had unnerved them they were about to rescue the half dead people that they had fought to save. Moments prior to the first poor souls being helped aboard, a wave, larger than any of them had ever witnessed before, hit the shipwreck. The sea crashed against the wreck's side, bodily skewing the 157 ton Estonian vessel beam onto them – and briefly displaying her salt encrusted name plate. The horrified lifeboat crew mouthed the letters into a word, *TOOGO*.

The wave shook the ship as if it was a toy. All of the people in the rigging were catapulted off and into the maelstrom, which surrounded the wreck – but alas, away from the waiting lifeboat. With the mountainous wave, the crippled schooner's decks were awash and the two people clinging to the mast vanished overboard. Adams's immediate reflex was to cut the anchor rope and set the main and mizzen sail. However, their exertions were instantly halted when they heard the piecing scream of a woman. The shriek was distinctive above the roar of the sea – and would haunt these poor men for years to come. It was the death-scream of the captain's wife as her terrifying ordeal came to an end. The startled crew looked upon their coxswain for guidance. Although he was duly affected by the woman's dying cry, he could not show his men any sign of weakness and shouted to them to carry on about their duties.

As they cleared the wreck of the *Toogo* he told them to keep a good lookout for those struggling in the sea. One of his crewmen thought he could hear cries close to the lurching *Charles Dibden* and, with mounting hope, they peered through the darkness. Nothing was seen, apart from wreckage, and Adams let his vessel drift with the flotsam, still hoping he would find some survivors.

When daybreak started to loom from the east, his men were exhausted and almost delirious with fatigue. It was only their conscience and sorrow which kept them uncomplaining and vigilant. In the first light they spied two men clinging desperately to an upturned dinghy a fair distance from the lifeboat. With the sea still just as rough they made six attempts to reach them. As they were about to make more adjustment to their sails, and another attempt, a   massive curling sea fell into the *Charles Dibden*. The lifeboat was equipped to shed the load of water by way of her self draining and non-return valves set into her deck.

Nonetheless, it had taken the crew unawares and coxswain Adams was thrown against one of the air boxes that were situated against the stern bulkhead. The violence of this assault drove the man's wind from his body. Before he could feel the hurt, he was nearly suffocated with the water and several crew members, who had also fallen on top of him.

His strength was starting to fail him and his back was in pain. The four men who had landed on him were lying on the deck with injuries – it was only his courage that made him carry on. He was now glad that he had had the foresight to take on two extra crewmen on this horrendous trip.

The two shipwrecked men were eventually pulled out of the water – more dead than alive. The lifeboat crew sympathetically administered first aid, but had difficulty in conversing with the Estonian sailors. With a swift scan of the sea around them, Will Adams saw no more survivors. He called to his tired, but relieved men that it was time to return to the lifeboat station and get proper care for the rescued men and injured crew.

The lifeboat surged heavily in the following seas, heeling and corkscrewing unpleasantly. Nonetheless, they were making quick progress home when Adams saw a steam ship requesting their attention. He reluctantly hove-to and the captain of the steamer *Woolpack* spoke to him through a loud hailer. He explained that they had rescued another man from the sea hours earlier. Miraculously it was a further survivor from the wreck of the *Toogo*. Wearily, Adams reasoned with the master that, in these sea conditions, it would be safer to leave the man aboard. The ship's captain agreed, and the relieved lifeboat coxswain again headed his craft for land.

As the *Charles Dibden* hit the beach a wave cascaded over her stern. Adams instinctively ducked as the water washed over him and the men. He flinched and grimaced as a pain seared through his back. Whilst the beach-crew was helping him out of his sturdy craft he was met by the anxious looking lifeboat secretary, John Prior. The request that Mr Prior made to Adams was, with regret, too much.* The lifeboat coxswain was escorted to a doctor, whose authority he had to obey, and was put straight to bed.

Nevertheless, the screams of the Estonian skipper's wife would always be there in his nightmares. He often wondered if it would have been different if the steamer had not delayed the rescue. Also, he felt that her master no doubt slept well and oblivious of the loss of life he had caused by his reckless action.

*See SEA OF SOULS

The North Deal lifeboat comes ashore

Corinthian's crew were hanging from the ratlines

SEA OF SOULS

Ernest Leek had been the captain of the ketch *Corinthian* for four months. The mate, George Green, was an 18 year old who had, for five years, learned his trade in barges. In the month that the young man had been aboard the vessel, Leek had got to know and like the youth. From the early age of 13, the mate, as had Leek, gained his experience from coastal trading in small craft – and was dedicated to his calling. There was a close-knit community of barge men and they were always well-informed of each other's whereabouts. Most of their ports of call were used by them all and they frequently passed within hailing distance on their voyages up and down the Channel.

Although many of the men started in humble barges, their promotion to the ketch barge induced a slight amount of snobbery amongst them. The ketch was in a different class to the numerous spritsail barges — she had a larger crew, numbering four or five, with ranks from captain and mate to able seaman (AB) and ordinary seaman. The only similarity with barges was the employment of a ship's boy. The big barges were seagoing vessels, around a hundred feet in length and the same in tons. Their sterns also had an elegant round counter unlike the square transom of the smaller craft. Their holds would be filled with approximately 150 to 200 tons of low cost cargoes, such as coal or building materials. Being more seaworthy they found many more shipments abroad than the estuary going barge.

On Friday morning, October 31st 1919, the *Corinthian* set sail in a freshening north-east breeze. The vessel, along with the slightly smaller ketch *Glenavon*, had completed loading phosphates in the port of Antwerp and they were sailing together for the Thames and London. Leek was happy that the 27 year old craft was not overloaded and the 160 tons of fertilizer did not impair her sea going qualities.

As the *Corinthian* left Antwerp, the captain and the mate discussed how they were going to share the four hour watches with the AB and ship's boy.

The AB was a seasoned hand. However, the boy, a sixteen year old from Hackney, in the east end of London, was on his first voyage. Leek was determined to keep his eye on the youngster. He had noted that the brash teenager had plenty to say for himself but he seemed to be a quick learner. A smile crept over the captain's face as he wondered how many clips around the ears the lad would receive, from the mate and AB, for any mistakes the boy made. He, however, would not tolerate any unnecessary bullying.

When they started to clear the shoal waters of the Belgian coastline, the wind freshened to a blustery east-north-east. At midday the wind strengthened to gale force and a sudden gust blew away the mizzen sail. In the worsening weather, Ernest Leek decided to make a run for it, to Dover.

Before they passed the *East Goodwin* lightship, the main sheet, a three inch thick manila rope which controlled the main boom, parted. It was seven o'clock in the evening and with the mainsail blowing out of control the *Corinthian* became unmanageable. Leek knew he was drifting on to the Goodwin Sands and was hastening to get a new cotton canvas mainsail ready to hoist. Minutes later they hit the sandbank.

In an instant the mizzen mast was ripped out and toppled overboard and the ketch started to take in water. Leek went below, gathered up some bedding and a paraffin lamp, and then hurried his crew aloft into the ratlines (cross ropes on the shrouds), which were attached to the main mast. As the seas swept her deck the *Corinthian* settled on to the Goodwins with only her mast showing above the raging sea.

After the captain had made sure that his meagre crew were secure in the rigging, he set light to the blankets. His signal of distress was quickly observed by the vigilant crew on the light vessels. At a quarter to ten, they started to fire rockets and their signal guns to alert those ashore.

From the shore the pyrotechnic display, from all three light ships, was a sight to behold in the darkness. This was going to be a tragic night to remember for Coxswain William Adams, as, forty-five minutes later, the North Deal lifeboat, *Charles Dibden*, crashed down the beach and into the surf. Little did the captain of the shipwrecked *Corinthian* know that he had summoned the lifeboat out to save lives from another craft in distress — the *Toogo*.

Leek waited in the rigging, occasionally shouting words of encouragement to his crew. The light vessels had stopped firing after they had received a response from the shore – he assured his men that it would only be a matter of time before they would be saved.

The hours went by. Every time a wave raked along the semi-submerged hull, the mast started to shake. With the main, fore and jib sail still set, these were jeopardizing the stability of the main mast. With every gust of wind the mast swayed dangerously.

Captain Leek felt the pangs of hunger; as they had not eaten since six that morning. Worst of all was the coldness which consumed their wet bodies. His desire for a smoke seemed to fill his mind – thankfully obliterating the thought that he may never see his wife and young son again.

Eight long bitter hours they suffered on. The ship's boy was in tears and no amounts of encouragement, which Leek shouted to him, helped. At six in the morning, the lad's ordeal came to an end. With a pitiful scream, he released his hold from the ratlines and plunged headlong into the fury of the waves and disappeared from sight. Sadness, as well as the biting wind, filled their eyes with tears. In despair, the master of the doomed ketch could not comprehend, why had they not been rescued by the lifeboat?

It was almost seven o'clock in the morning when the *Charles Dibden* came ashore, in a flurry of spray. The coxswain William Adams was helped out of his craft, along with the two rescued seamen from the *Toogo*. John Prior, the lifeboat secretary and agent for the Shipwrecked Mariners Society, informed the weary Adams that more wrecks had been sighted. In the weak light of dawn two shipwrecks were visible on the skyline amidst the grey swirling sea. Adams's heart fell, however, he was in such pain, from the injury that he had sustained in the lifeboat, he knew he could not render further assistance. Prior reluctantly appealed to William Stanton, the reserve lifeboat coxswain, to re-launch the *Charles Dibden* and assist the casualties.

Poor Stanton was gravely ill with throat cancer and was awaiting entry into hospital for an operation. He did not falter in his reply and called out for fresh volunteers to take the life-belts of those injured or fatigued. At seven-thirty the boat ploughed back into the waves; it would be Stanton's last ever lifeboat rescue. There was no let up in the weather, and to those ashore, with wind sweeping up the beach, it seemed to be getting worse.

With their hands numb, Captain Leek helped secure the other two crewmen on to the ratlines with rope from the rigging. The mate was barely conscious and was delirious with exhaustion. As the captain strained his bloodshot eyes over the horizon for deliverance, he came across the sad sight of the other ketch *Glenavon*. The vessel was in a similar predicament to them, with all of crew hanging on to the rigging.

Meanwhile, the lifeboat was making heavy going beating into the wind. It was to take seven hours for them to cover the six and a half miles to reach the distant *Corinthian*.

By ten, that morning, Leek saw the last of the crew disappear from the wreck of the *Glenavon*. By now there was little conversation amongst his hypothermic men. Their will to live was fading fast. As they clung to the fragile main mast, Leek still scanned the bleak spume filled sea for salvation. It eventually came in the vision of the *Charles Dibden*, rolling violently below them. Ernest Leek's first concern was for his mate, the young George Green. His condition was becoming critical and Leek urged him to tie the rope, which was cast from the lifeboat, about himself. With the remaining strength the man had, he laboriously looped the rope under his arms and secured it with a bowline knot. The fatigued captain then commanded him to release his hold on the ratlines to enable the lifeboat crew to pull him to safety. Green's nerves were at breaking point. With what little courage he had left, he let go of the rope ladder that had supported him over the last 17 hours. As the lifeboat crew hauled the mate towards them, he came foul of a thick rope shroud which was bracing up the main mast. The unfortunate man's mind finally snapped and he held on to the rope in a death grip.

No matter how much the lifeboat men pleaded with him to let go, he would not obey. Leek even risked his own life by climbing down to him and then tried to prise the poor man's fingers apart. With sadness the captain left him as he died – with salvation mere yards away.

The AB and Leek were assisted into the rolling *Charles Dibden* and, after another 25 minutes of pulling, the battered dead body of the mate was hauled aboard. The ketch's captain explained that the crew of the *Glenavon* had perished earlier and Coxswain Stanton decided to make for shore with all due haste.

· On that dismal afternoon, at half past three, the lifeboat was winched up the beach. As the survivors of the *Corinthian* were ushered into the near-by public house, 'The Forrester', for dry clothes and a hot drink, Ernest Leek met the agent for Shipwrecked Mariners, John Prior – little did he know that he would make his acquaintance again, four years later, when this brave man was once more rescued by the lifeboat.*

*See 'TALES FROM AROUND THE GOODWIN SANDS' page 45.

The remains of the steam ship *Falcon*

SPONTANEOUS COMBUSTION

The *Falcon* was old and she was ugly. Her 50 years afloat had not been kind to the old girl and she had almost been worked to death. Normally a steam ship of that age would have been delivered to the breakers many years past. However, her owners, General Steam Navigation Company, wanted to get their last pound of flesh from her.

Not being a large vessel she was put on a coastal run, hopping over to France and Belgium with general cargoes. Some thought that she was lucky, in the middle of the First World War, not to have been put out of her misery when a torpedo was fired at her and missed. Indeed they thought it a miracle that the U boat captain neglected to kill such an easy target. Sarcastically, they surmised the German must have misjudged her speed.

Sunday 24th October, 1926, saw the steamer plodding back to London from the Port of Ostende. Not only were her holds full but also part of her general cargo was stowed on the deck.

At 10 in the morning, the *Falcon* was passing the outside edge of the North Goodwins. The steward had just taken a turn on deck before he laid up the crew's lunch table. He noted that the weather was starting to turn nasty and the wind was freshening. As he made his way back along the companionway, he smelled smoke. This was not dirty coal smoke from the funnel but a smouldering odour. On investigation he saw that a bale of jute, stowed in the alleyway, had spontaneously combusted.

Before the alarm could be raised the wind whipped the fire into a blaze.

Lunch was soon forgotten as the crew tried to put the fire out. Unfortunately, it had spread to the rest of the bales of jute and the heat drove them back. Smoke choked the men and they quickly collected their possessions from their quarters amidships.

The bridge and accommodation had been set alight and smoke was billowing from the centre of the ship. Captain Acors directed the engineers to stop the vessel from going ahead but still wanted enough steam to be maintained to drive the fire pumps.

Attracted by the smoke, several other ships stood-by the burning steamer. It was one of them that radioed the coast guards of the mishap.

The crew aboard the *Falcon* struggled with the situation — not only were the pumps being used but men were also employing buckets of sea water trying to put out the inferno. Suddenly the forward cargo hold erupted. Part of the ship's load had been 10,000 cases of matches.

Falcon's captain realised the fire was getting out of hand and also becoming a danger to his crew. After he had mustered all of the men he reluctantly lowered the ship's lifeboat and made sure they all got on board. One of the steamers standing by, the *Elswick House*, soon picked them up.

Whilst the rescued crew were having lunch and a rest on the *Elswick House* the Ramsgate lifeboat and the Dover tug *Lady Brassey* arrived. With smoke-smudged faces and still chewing on their meal, these sailors were herded into the lifeboat.

Falcon was due for retirement

Captain Acors viewed his ship. The fire was burning fiercely but had not spread. He asked to be put back onboard the *Falcon*, although the lifeboat coxswain had advised against it.

When the captain of the tug felt there was a possibility of salvage, it was decided that another attempt should be tried to save the old ship. Upwind to the derelict, the lifeboat carefully nudged up to her stern. Acors, along with the second mate, chief engineer and two lifeboat crewmen were reunited with the blazing ship.

They hastily made sure the hand steering gear was functional and then they were transferred by the lifeboat to the bow and secured the tow. Slowly the tug towed the ship to the south-west and into the strengthening wind. As they past the South Goodwins the bridge and crews quarters collapsed in a mass of flames.

At half past seven, the night sky off Dover Harbour was lit up. The fire was consuming the highly inflammable cargo and there would be no chance of putting it out. Port control at Dover Harbour decided that it could not risk allowing this floating furnace into their haven and refused entry.

The tug, *Lady Brassey*, reluctantly towed the *Falcon* back out to sea. With the heat, the old ship was starting to split close to the waterline. Three miles offshore, at nine fifteen, the tow rope snapped. The crew on the tug saw that the *Falcon's* iron hull plates were glowing red with the heat. It was decided to abandon the vessel as it would only be a matter of time before she sank. They returned to the harbour as the wind picked up to gale force with driving rain.

Men on the Eastern Entrance of Dover Harbour kept a watch on the flaming ship. The rain had not lessened the blaze – that was being assisted by the strong wind. As they watched, they realised that the gale was driving the derelict fire ship closer towards them. By this time the sea had become too rough for the tug to attend.

Slowly but surely the lurching *Falcon* was being drawn towards the harbour. Most of the cargo had been burnt – however, there was still an impressive display of flames coming from her hold. Closer and closer the wind drove the burning pyre.

The tide and the gale created a maelstrom off the Eastern Arm and large waves buffeted off the harbour wall. This was enough to prevent the *Falcon* from entering and she slowly drifted on to the shoreline. At midnight, on the top of a high spring tide, the ship was almost dashed into the cliff face. In a welter of scalding steam and smoke waves pushed the vessel around broadside – extinguishing the fire and filling her holds with water and shingle.

When the dawn cast its first light the wreck was still smoking. The main fire had been put out yet the cargo still smouldered. The blackened hull was in stark contrast with the white cliffs. Fortunately the gale force wind had subsided enough for a salvage crew to be put ashore from a motor boat. Onlookers had also made their way down Langdon Stairs, opposite the wreck, and were surveying the scene.

They were met with an unpromising view. The hull had split in two places and the accommodation and deck were completely burnt away. All of the superstructure, the two masts and aft crane had collapsed into the burnt-out ship – only the forward crane remained standing. The iron plates around her midships were buckled, with the heads of the rivets melted away. Incredibly, the smoke stained Red Ensign was still flying from the flag pole aft.

The remains of the charred cargo were not worth the bother of removing. Salvors deemed that the 50 year old hull had no financial value and, after some scrap iron had been disposed of, the *Falcon* was to be left in situ to rot.

At every high tide she would disappear, only to re-appear as the sea receded. Over the years her iron plates and ribs have taken longer to rust away than if she had been made from steel. Eventually the sea has eroded the *Falcon* down to her keel and bilge. Even to this day, at low water, the sad remains of the hulk can be viewed at the bottom of the Langdon Stairs. She is a relic of a bygone age of steam – yet her rusting skeleton has outlasted many of her modern contemporaries.

View of the wreck from the Langdon Stairs

Peter Hawksfield entering Dover Harbour

'AS THICK AS GUTS'

'As thick as guts' is an expression many seamen use to describe the phenomenon of dense fog. Sea-mist, which turns into fog, is caused by the water temperature clashing with the air temperature. This weather condition could happen at any time – and in the days before radar was invented it was the dread of every sailor. Unlike a storm, men in ships could not by their own actions weather it or shelter from it. No matter how much sea-room you had, there was always going to be a chance that someone else would be on a collision course with your vessel. Fog would mean the loss of man's greatest sense – that of sight.

Hawksfield & Son was a successful and well known coal merchant of Dover and had the concession to supply coal to the port for the steamers to bunker. It was so successful that the company had their own ships, *Peter Hawksfield* and *Kathleen Hawksfield*. These vessels could carry the cargoes of coal from the pits in the north of England directly to their yards at Dover.

One such consignment was being ferried from Blythe to Dover, when a thick sea mist descended on 24th March 1938. The *Peter Hawksfield* was a fairly old ship that had two previous owners since she was built in 1918. The coal merchant had bought her nine years before and she had been a 'regular', unloading coal at Dover docks throughout those years. She was less than a 1,000 gross registered tons and carried a crew of 12, plus the skipper. Being on coastal voyages was no great hardship for the men and they appreciated not being away from their families for too long.

The *Peter Hawksfield* was proceeding through the Downs, off Deal, when she was enveloped in a fog bank. With 6 miles to go, Captain McNab did not fancy the idea of navigating through the fog-bound harbour entrance at Dover. He decided to anchor up and wait for the fog to lift.

Most of the crew busied themselves in their claustrophobic accommodations, and some got their bags together for disembarkation in a few hours time. Once they were home they could put the tin bath in front of the fire and wash the coal dust from their bodies; they could read the newspaper, go to the pub or just spend some time with their loved ones before they went back to sea again on the next coal run. Around them the fog shrouded the ship, cold and clammy. Apart from their regulation fog signal, the only other sound was the sea washing against the anchored ship's hull.

The same chill Channel mist had crept down around the 12,436 ton Shaw Savill & Albion liner *Wairangi* as she entered the Downs. The massive three year old ship could carry not only passengers but also vast amounts of cargo.

As the mist turned into thick fog, her master realised the destruction that a vessel of this size could do at 17 knots. He reduced his speed down to a minimum and put an extra man on watch in her bow.

The helmsman was too busy staring at the compass to notice the bow look-outs frantically waving their arms. When the large ship shuddered slightly he looked up and the captain ordered 'stop engines'.

The bows of the *Wairangi* had pierced the fragile hull of the *Peter Hawksfield* on her starboard side just forward of the bridge. Even at slow speed, the impact of the passenger ship's bow penetrated the collier's hull five or six feet – sufficient to force her deck beams through to the port side of the ship. With the high pitched noise of tearing metal, the *Peter Hawksfield's* bridge was ripped from the deck and fell into the sea.

At a quarter to two on that dismal Thursday afternoon, all was silent. Shock and astonishment showed on everybody's face. Thankfully, and miraculously, there had not been any fatal casualties. One of the liner's officers was the first to order a rope ladder to be cast down onto the mangled deck of the collier. The captain of the *Wairangi* alerted the North Foreland by radio and they in turn called for the Walmer lifeboat to be put on standby. Thick fog still cloaked the whole area.

The men on the *Peter Hawksfield* soon collected their wits. They could see their ship was only being kept afloat by the embrace of this enormous liner's bow. Below the ragged and torn deck, they could see the sea – the bow of the liner had almost torn their ship in half. Quickly and without panic they climbed the rope ladder that was hanging from the *Wairangi*. In their haste they did not even have time to collect any of their personal belongings.

Suddenly the *Peter Hawksfield* started to buckle and the noise of ripping steel again filled their ears. As the last man was assisted over the side, the *Wairangi* slowly pulled astern from the collier, her bow hardly showing any signs of damage. The small ship sounded as if she was giving a sigh of relief when the air escaped from her crippled hull, and she slipped beneath the sea in ten fathoms of water. The fog was still 'as thick as guts' but now, ten minutes after the collision, it only masked one ship.

Another radio message from the *Wairingi* went to shore to explain that all hands on the *Peter Hawksfield* had been saved. The crew of the Walmer lifeboat were gratefully stood down. They were not looking forward to navigating through the thick murk which had not only engulfed the sea but also the lifeboat station and most of the sea front.

A day after the collision, Trinity House sent out three of their vessels to try to locate the wreck. The conditions prevailed, which added to their difficulty, nonetheless, they found a wreck and positioned two buoys to mark the site.

However, the position that Trinity House gave was not where the remains of the *Peter Hawksfield* lay. Strangely it was another unknown and uncharted First World War casualty – although very close to the remnants of the collier.

Over the years the position of the '*Hawksfield*' was discovered and she became a popular dive for the scuba diving fraternity. One diver wandered off the site and found a gun which on closer inspection was found to be a 3-pounder, Admiralty number 344. It would be enough proof that there were two wrecks very close together and the divers realised that it could not have come off a collier sunk in 1938. Both of the wrecks were mangled and almost un-recognisable, nevertheless, they still stood on the seabed as monuments of past tragedies.

U-16 on sea-trials

DEATH OF A U-BOAT

In war brave men die on both sides. Each country's warriors fight for what they feel is right, nevertheless men still die.

When Britain declared war on Germany in 1939, she was not ready or equipped for the onslaught that was to follow. The Nazi war machine was prepared and brought its might into action immediately. Even so, Britain had the courage to counteract the assault.

The Royal Navy knew the Straits of Dover would take the initial brunt of the action, as they had done in the First World War. The mines had been a menace then and, with new technology, would be a greater one than ever before. In the first few months it would be the mine that accounted for much of the lost marine tonnage. Apart from the ss *Athenia* being torpedoed by the *U-30* within hours of the start of the conflict, most of the German U-boats were deployed in laying these deadly seeds where they would hurt most. The Downs would be one such area, along with the shipping routes towards the River Thames.

Having been useful in the first conflict, the Admiralty decided to employ trawlers once again. The converted trawlers did the best they could by sweeping the shipping channels clear. There was also a need for extra anti-submarine vessels – which the navy did not have. The answer to this problem would be to cut holes cut through the hulls of the requisitioned deep sea trawlers and fit asdic tubes through them. The necessary electronic equipment was installed and men were rapidly trained to use it. Decks of the trawlers had to be reinforced to take the racks and the extra weight of depth charges.

Another way of detecting the enemy, was by laying an anti-submarine indicator loop. This was enabled by the production of an induced current in a stationary monitored loop of wire. When a U-boat passed above the loop it produced a small current from the boat's magnetic properties. One of these loops was placed in Kellet Gut, a seldom used channel running between the north and south banks of the Goodwin Sands. This was monitored from the coast guard station at Deal.

It was a stormy night on 24th October 1939, and the gale that was blowing against the windows of the wooden coast guard station was keeping the men watchful. When the dials on the anti-submarine loop indicated a presence they were quick to notify the Admiralty at Dover. From this warning, the Dover Commander in Chief alerted the vessels *Cayton Wyke* and *Puffin* of the situation.

The *Cayton Wyke* was a large, converted deep sea Hull trawler of 373 tons that had been sold to the Admiralty a month before. On her foredeck stood a 12 pounder and in the stern were full racks of depth-charges. Accompanying her was the patrol vessel H.M.S. *Puffin*. She was a purpose-built naval ship of the Kingfisher class and had all the armaments of war fitted as standard. Within an hour, the two vessels came upon the area close to the Goodwins with their asdic pinging the seabed in search of the foe.

Asdic searches in the Downs were always unpopular with the operators. With so many wrecks on the seabed, it was difficult to discern an inert lump of rusting metal from a U-boat. Many a time depth charges were wasted – only to be discovered that an unwary and embarrassed skipper had spent too long destroying what was already destroyed. Nonetheless, on this night the two naval vessels increased their speed and started their depth charge run as soon as they entered the region of the Kellet Gut.

It was a dark and foul night and Kapitanleutnant Horst Wellner had not realised the *U-16* had been detected.

U-16 had left Kiel six days earlier and had successfully laid a mine field off Dungeness. Why Wellner had steered his submarine through the Goodwins into the Downs will always be a mystery. Perhaps he was trying to emulate the accomplishment of the *U-12*, 25 years earlier, when she sunk H.M.S. *Niger* at the start of the First World War.* Whatever his reasons were, they will never be known.

High and dry on the Goodwins

The two anti-submarine vessels hulls vibrated with the maximum revolutions that the engineers could obtain from their engines. If their speed could not be maintained they knew they would become a victim of their own depth charges. On a command, both vessels dropped a depth charge that had been adjusted to explode at 60 feet. The splash that they made was hardly noticeable in the wake of the ships, then, suddenly, the sea burst into a mass of white. The *Cayton Wyke* and *Puffin* shuddered with the explosions, their sterns lifting slightly.

Again and again depth charges rained down into the sea. The ships' crews' adrenalin was running high with the chase. They hardly noticed the rough Channel chop that the gale was stirring up or even the loud explosions that were occurring.

Into the early hours of the morning, those ashore at Deal who had been awoken by the initial explosions, counted a total of 82 dull thuds.

When the ships exhausted their racks of depth charges, both vessels communicated with each other. Lieutenant Commander Waldegrave of H.M.S. *Puffin*, advised Chief Skipper Noble, from the *Cayton Wyke* that it was time to abandon the hunt. He knew that it would have been an achievement to have captured the U-boat, nevertheless, they had done their best. There were no outward signs of a kill and it was best to vacate the area until daybreak. As they left, the surface of the sea in the Downs was littered with thousands of dead fish.

Kapitanleutnant Wellner and his crew had survived the barrage. The detonations had been close to the U-boat, but none close enough to collapse the pressure hull. The men had endured what had seemed a life-time encapsulated in a claustrophobic steel tomb. The noise had deafened them and the U-boat had been rocked with every blast. They felt lucky to have survived – however, the harm had been done. Wellner knew his *U-16* had been damaged sufficiently for them not to be able to escape back to the Fatherland. The explosions had shattered the engine mounts and steering and the crew's nerves were also shattered. He managed to surface his craft and make a hasty wireless message back to base that he was about to scuttle the *U-16*. It was the last that was ever heard from those men on that dark and stormy night. What happened after that nobody will ever know. The only thing that is clear, is that 28 men died. Some bodies were found weeks later washed up on the French shore – one of them being Horst Wellner.

The 140 foot semi-submerged hull of the *U-16* was washed around the Goodwins all of the next day unnoticed, apart from the occasional curious seagull. Her insides had been sabotaged by the fleeing crew and her secret papers destroyed. There was just sufficient buoyancy to float her up on to the south part of the sandbank.

The following day, the gale had subdued enough for some Deal boatmen to get afloat. They briefly witnessed the derelict hull high and dry on the Goodwins. *U-16* looked like a stranded whale with the black backed gulls, known to the boatmen as 'corpse eaters', wheeling above the open hatch in the conning tower. Before the Sands could embrace her, the tide lifted the submarine once more and rolled her around in the mercy of its flow. As it ebbed, the U-boat slid down the most southern side of the bank and disappeared from sight forever.

Four months later, it was written in Dover's secret orders that a survey had found 'a first class echo, typical of a submarine on the bottom lying north-west to south-east.' The position given was on the south side edge of the Goodwin Sands in 70 feet of water.

The *Cayton Wyke* and H.M.S. *Puffin* were acknowledged for the kill. The Admiralty trawler went on to assist in the Dunkirk evacuation and carried on with her duties with the Dover Patrol. Unfortunately, she was pounced on and torpedoed by a German E-boat in September 1940, close to the inner side of the Goodwins. The audacious attack by the *S-36* was enough to sink her about half-a-mile from the remains of the *U-16*. As *Cayton Wyke* sank, she capsized and ended upside-down on the sea-bed, with her asdic tube jutting out obscenely from her upturned hull.

H.M.S. *Puffin* almost survived the war unscathed. On 26th March 1945, off the coast of Lowestoft, the patrol vessel sighted an enemy *Seehund* mini-submarine on the surface. Without a moment's hesitation, the captain steered *Puffin* on a collision course toward the *Seehund*. On impact, the two torpedoes slung under the two-man submarine's hull exploded. Of the *Seehund* nothing was found, however, *Puffin* sustained severe damage to her bow. She was towed back and spent what was left of the war laid-up and irreparable.

The loss of the *U-16* taught the Germans to be more cautious with their precious submarines. Within the same month of the *U-16's* demise, the *U-12* and *U-40* were also sunk in the Dover Straits. The importance of the mines did not lessen and they were still laid nightly – only this time by German aircraft.

* See 'TALES FROM AROUND THE GOODWIN SANDS' page33

Cayton Wyke before the Admiralty converted her into an anti-submarine vessel

The white band around her hull and funnel was painted out in Gibraltar

AN EXTRAORDINARY COINCIDENCE

The Brocklebank Line *Mahratta*, which was lost on the Goodwin Sands in 1909, was a famous local shipwreck. There was even a series of photographic postcards of the wreck which were sold to holidaymakers by their hundreds. The masts from the hulk survived above the waves long enough for every man, woman and child in Deal to know her name. Some of the mahogany furniture from her passengers' cabins is still used in a few of the homes in the area to this day. The 446 foot long hull, which Harland and Wolfe had built in 1892, found the Goodwins chalk subsurface and the bulk of the ship could not be swallowed by the sand.

It would be a very extraordinary coincidence to believe that another ship, of the same name and belonging to the same company, could have been lost within three-quarters of a mile from her sister ship. Nevertheless, 30 years after the first event, the second ship met her fate.

On 6th October 1939, the anchorage in the Downs was crowded with vessels waiting to be checked by the Contraband Patrol. Once they were cleared they could proceed under the orders of a naval officer. He would direct them on a safe route which would take them through the mine swept shipping channel.

The *Mahratta* was one such ship. She had left Calcutta before the war had begun – en-route to Colombo, Port Sudan, Port Said and Gibraltar. Whilst picking up cargo, she became engulfed in Hitler's hostilities and it was at Gibraltar that she received her war colours. The 22 inch broad, white banded line which went around the top of her hull was blackened out – this would hopefully deter the enemy from identifying her company and name. Her cargo comprised of hundreds of tons of tea, jute and hemp – much the same as her predecessor carried in 1909.

Captain Hill had received orders to proceed with the *Mahratta* to London. He viewed the Downs with interest as he had never seen so many ships in such a small area before. As dusk fell, the ships dimly illuminated their presence; it looked as if there was a small city afloat. Hill knew he needed a pilot onboard to help con his vessel to Gravesend – but being impatient to get on, he slowly nudged his 6,690 ton ship through the congested anchorage.

Aboard his cutter, the Trinity House Pilot, Tod Carlton, was motoring in the darkness from ship to ship, trying to find his charge. As the *Mahratta* had moved from where she had been anchored, Captain Carlton was having difficulty in locating her.

With the closely moored up vessels in her way, the *Mahratta* eased her helm out towards the east and, unbeknown to Captain Hill, towards the Goodwins. The sea was so calm they hardly felt the bump when the ship came to a halt. Hill had a slightly puzzled look on his face as he asked his chief engineer what was wrong with the engine as they were not making headway.

The pilot eventually came across the stranded vessel on part of the Goodwins known as the Fork Spit. He assessed the situation and knew nothing could be done until daylight. The following day, six tugs were brought down from Gravesend to assist; also hired were two Deal motor boats to survey the depth of water around the trapped ship. The skippers of these small craft had seen it all before, yet they kept their opinions to themselves. They helped transfer the tugs hawsers to the *Mahratta* for an attempt to pull the ship off at high tide. However, the tugs efforts were in vain, as they failed to tow the vessel off the Sands.

For the next three high tides the tugs strove in their labours. The weather was starting to take precedence of the situation and winds of gale-force ferocity were blowing from the south-east. Eventually the tugs managed to move the ship into slightly deeper water, but being neap tides there was still not enough below *Mahratta's* keel to float her off. On the 10th October she was stranded inelegantly broadside across the tide, her bows pointing to the east.

The *Mahratta* did not last long on the Goodwins

Captain Hill was now getting worried. After consultation with his 15 officers and the tug skippers, it was agreed that the ship should be lightened. Hill's officers organized part of his Lascar crew to haul 210 tons of jute from the holds to be dumped overboard. Two large admiralty lighters were towed up from Dover and were secured alongside the stranded vessel. In the early hours of the morning, rasping noises were heard – the ship was starting to buckle. The Goodwins was reluctant to relinquish her catch.

The Indian crew were the first to get agitated as the sounds grew louder. Deal boatmen who were hovering around the wreck noticed some of the ship's plates, with the rust and paint flaking off, crinkling. An occasional bang made men start, as a rivet broke and sounded like a rifle shot. The salvage crew realised that they did not have much time left.

Word was sent ashore to the Deal boatmen for help with the salvage. It was agreed that anything saved would be paid one third of its value. Plywood chests of tea were the most accessible items and these boxes were stacked into the small boats until it was impossible to see the bow from the stern. Ashore, there were 130 cases of tea stored on the sea-front, to the north of Deal pier. However, in the darkness of night a lot of tea seemed to evaporate into thin air. The customs officials realised that something was amiss. It only needed a rumour that there were going to be raids and, once again, as had happened 30 years past, the drains of Deal were blocked with dumped, swollen, wet tea.

The *Mahratta,* being broadside onto the tide, was now suffering from the sand being scoured fore and aft. This was increasing the hogging of the keel and the ship was breaking her back quicker than the men could salvage her cargo. The rifle shot bangs of the rivets breaking were increasing into the staccato of a machine-gun. With a loud report, the large ship broke in half.

The *Mahratta's* deck gaped in two halves. Amidst the rush of escaping steam from the boilers, a crewman died. The main steam pipes had been closed down, nevertheless there was enough engine steam left to work the ship's derricks – which allowed the unloading of the cargo. With the ship juddering and the rush of escaping steam the Lascar sailors panicked. The captain gave permission for them to be evacuated from the ship. Two of the Deal boats, *Lady Haig* and *Skipjack* ferried the 70 crew, 16 officers and a passenger to a waiting tug. The ordeal was over; the ship was lost and the Goodwin Sands had claimed yet another everlasting victim.

In between the winter weather, various pieces of cargo were reclaimed – either washed ashore or taken from whichever part of the wreck was still above the water. Within weeks, the sea and sand swallowed her leaving only the masts showing. Because she was a British merchantman, her demise was heavily censured; it was not advisable to advertise – to the enemy – merchant tonnage lost by carelessness.

The semi-submerged hulk created one or two frights with new unsuspecting skippers of navy patrol boats. With the hull just showing above the waves, their first reaction was that they had discovered a U-boat. Others, who were more familiar with the wreck, used it for target practice.

During the 1960s, the wreck was claimed to have been bought from the insurance company by a local individual. He attempted a small amount of salvage and managed to lift part of the *Mahratta's* massive phosphorus bronze propeller. It was a precarious operation with the prop hanging from the stem of the *Gay Dolphin*. This boat was only 25 feet long and her bow's were almost under as she motored away with it.

Nowadays, the only disturbance the *Mahratta* gets is from the fishermen. With the sunken hull facing across the tide, the current disturbs the sand eels which, in turn, then attract the sought after sea bass. She has become a famous hot-spot for the anglers and the ship's name is, yet again, perpetuated.

Merchant ships being boarded by the Contraband Control

44

Nora's bottom became exposed to all and sundry

LOCAL KNOWLEDGE

Before Nazi Germany could extend her invading tentacles throughout all of Europe, the neutral ships had to display their nationality. The country's flag and name was painted upon their hulls – hopefully to deter a U-boat captain from making a mistake and creating an international incident. However, at sea, mines had no such ethics.

Throughout January 1940, the Downs was busy with the Contraband Control tugs going about their business checking the cargoes of the neutral vessels. Each and every night, the droning engines of German aircraft could be heard near-by. They were dropping mines close to the anchorage with impunity. The weather was bitterly cold and gales would blow up without warning. It was always the fear of the anchored ships' officers and crew that these mines might break loose in the rough seas and indiscriminately select a victim.

Many of the local boatmen did not need the nationality embezzled on the hulls to know their port of origin. They could identify where the ship came from by the shape of the hull and superstructure.

Once these vessels were cleared by the Contraband Control they would then await authorization from the Royal Naval officers. These officers appeared to be over officious, to many, and were greatly disliked by the longshoremen. They restricted their movements with red tape and bureaucracy – an imposition that the Deal men were not used to – and they became outwardly defiant towards them. With the threat of invasion, Deal was deemed to be an obvious landing area for the Germans. Steel defence girders appeared along the sea-front to deter and contain any of the invading forces. Unfortunately, this restricted the boatmen's rights of passage further.

Early on Monday morning January 29th the small Dutch scoot, *Nora,* lay uncomfortable at anchor in a southerly swell. She was only 298 gross registered tons and had a cargo of 317 tons of straw boards. Her voyage from the port of Harlinger had been a rough one and she was temporary berthed in the Small Downs anchorage, awaiting clearance orders to sail to London. Snow had been falling steadily all night and had covered the little coaster's deck. The motor vessel holds were tightly battened down against the inclement weather and some of the crew huddled into the confines of the wheelhouse, drinking coffee. Although the seamen were used to the cold, they felt as though their blood and stamina had thinned somewhat with the thought of the weapons of war that surrounded them. The mines, being the unknown factor, played on their fears. Anything that could be seen, could be avoided, however, what lurked beneath the surface was terrifying. To the seamen it was like sitting on a time-bomb.

Along with the *Nora*, anchored a mile offshore, were many other ships. The majority were far larger than her and the *Nora's* crew took some relief in believing that, if there were any magnetic mines around, these ships would be more susceptible than themselves.

The strong ebb tide was slackening and the southerly wind was picking up when a contact mine brushed against the *Nora's* stern. In the galley, the cook took the brunt of the explosion. The stern of the little ship was lifted out of the water and the galley was demolished. Pots, pans and the cooking stove were momentarily suspended in the air as they were wrenched from their brackets. A large hole appeared and the cook, in the confusion, only just managed to crawl to safety as the cold sea poured in.

In the wheelhouse, Captain Brinkman and the mate staggered backwards as the glass from the windows burst inwards. Blood was splattered around the binnacle and wheel as the deadly shards ripped into the Dutchmen's faces. They staggered about blinded and dazed.

Meanwhile, the seaman who had been making his way towards the wheelhouse was catapulted off the slippery deck and into the cold grey sea. The hole that the mine had made was large and the jagged ends had imploded into the inside of the hull. At this moment the *Nora* quickly started to sink by the stern.

Two Admiralty tugs sped to the strickened ship to enable them to take off the wounded men. As the coaster tilted and sank lower in the water, extreme urgency assaulted their senses. The *Nora's* engineer, who was the captain's brother, assisted the British sailors in saving the crew and it was found that the cook was the most severely injured. He could not stand, as the blast had fractured his legs, and along with this he had taken a beating with the flying pots and pans. The captain and mate were unrecognisable, blood covered their faces and clothing – nevertheless, they were still standing. The Dutch engineer searched the small craft for the missing seaman, but gave up on the command of the tug's captain. The hypothermic but fortunate man was rescued from the sea half an hour later by a patrol vessel.

The tugs hastily secured wire hawsers to the *Nora*, which had seemed to have maintained some buoyancy – possibly because the cargo of straw boards was keeping her afloat. Then they towed her towards the shoreline, close to Deal Castle, and, with great difficulty, she was beached upon the foreshore.

The local boatmen watched this manoeuvre with shaking heads. A couple of old salts remonstrated with the naval officer who had seemed to have taken charge. They told him that the spring tide was making and a southerly gale was starting to blow. The lieutenant looked at the longshoremen in bewilderment and scorn. Again, they tried to reason with the arrogant fellow. They stated that high tide would be in two hours time, at twenty minutes past two, and with the gale of wind it would sweep the wreck off the beach and on to the pier. With an outward show of distain, the officer dismissed the men and sought shelter from the freezing conditions.

In amongst the flurries of snow, the seafront became crowded with locals looking at the new addition to the beach. They watched as the tide made and started to cover the half sunken hulk. The southerly gale helped the surf crash up on to the beach and then swept the shingle away from the high water mark. The hulk of the *Nora* started to move with the violence of the surf – she slowly bobbed with each wave and then drew off in the backwash.

The flood tide had got a hold of her, and, with the wind, the half submerged ship started to roll towards Deal pier. By now the sea-front was crowded with hundreds of on-lookers braving the cold to get a front row view. The boatmen mingled with the locals and relayed, to those interested, that their warnings to the Admiralty personnel had gone unheeded. Many of the people agreed that the authorities should have taken more notice of the boatmen, as they had local knowledge.

With an audible crash, which was heard above the roar of the gale, metal grated against metal as the *Nora* hit the pier.

At first, it halted the progress of the ship and a brave pier attendant looked down at her as she surged in the surf. It took up to six collisions before the first pile of the Victorian pier gave way and the attendant made a hasty retreat. Acting as a giant battering ram, the ship pounded the remaining pier piles until she made a breach through to the other side.

The tide was starting to fall and the *Nora* bounced on the bottom in the surf. Just 50 feet north of the mangled pier she rolled over on her side and, as the sea receded further, settled into the shingle. At low tide the following day, Admiralty surveyors clambered over the hull, which was displaying the painted Dutch flag skywards,

Nora's original name

and declared her as a total loss. Tons of shingle entered the hulk and settled it further down into the beach – this time she did not move.

With the threat of invasion, the authorities declared that the *Nora* had saved them the job of demolishing the pier to stop any landings that could have been made by the enemy. Even some of the boatmen secretly had no regrets with its destruction; they and their fathers had disliked its construction as it hampered their sailing boats and restricted the shot of their drifting sprat nets.

The hulk was resented by many of the local householders. They had had to give up their front railings and other iron implements to help the war effort – yet there on the beach were tons of stranded steel.

After the war, in 1947, the Deal town council felt they had to do something about the eyesore. Being on the beach and close to property, the Admiralty could not destroy it by their usual method – explosives. The rusting wreck was sold as scrap and cut up in situ and – much to the disgust of local anglers and the youthful locals who used it as a summer diving platform – carted away.

In 1974 a local scuba diver, Johnny Rees, discovered the bell from the meagre remains of the shipwreck. There was some confusion until it was realised that the name of **'BERENT'** inscribed on the bell was the *Nora's* previous name.

Sailors have always deemed the renaming of a ship to be unlucky, perhaps the renaming of the *Nora* proved a point!

Heavy daytime losses of Flying Fortress's were encountered

MISS LOLLIPOP

The summer months of 1944 were to be a most crucial time in World War Two. Secret plans for the invasion of Europe were well advanced and the Allied forces had prepared for the 'big push'. Men, armament and supplies were being brought over the Atlantic in purpose-built cargo ships. Meteorologists strived to find a calm window in the unsettled weather patterns and bomber command was subtly softening up Nazi installations which could hamper the advancing troops of D-Day.

America was pulling out all of the stops, and without their help the war would have carried on longer than necessary – and more lives would have been needlessly lost. The brand new equipment that was being shipped over from the United States was up-to-date and high-tech.

Germany was almost on her knees, but continued to doggedly fight on against all odds.

New B17-g Flying Fortress aircraft costing $247,000 before being equipped for war, were landing in their hundreds at airfields around England. The 10-hour flight across the Atlantic Ocean would show up any small mechanical defects which the ground crew could fix within hours of landing.

On 26th May 1944, the B17 *Miss Lollipop*, so named because one of the manufacturers employees's felt she would be a 'good ship', had just received her new American crew of 10. They were based at Thorpe Abbotts, Norfolk, with the 349th Bombardment Squadron of the 100th Bombardment Group. Being part of the 8th Air Force, they were nick-named the 'Bloody Hundredth'. Their losses were high and, in 1943, the average life expectancy of an air crew was 11 missions.

Although the bombers were encountering fewer enemy engagements over occupied territory, their day flights always attracted some resistance. The early morning of the 12th June, 1944, saw a major bombing run into Northern France. The D-Day invasion was six

48

days old and their mission was to destroy the enemy's rail and communication network.

Miss Lollipop, in formation with a large flight of other Flying Fortresses, was leaving a vapour trail at 26,000 feet. The raid had been successfully accomplished, however, the B17's bomb bay doors would not close. Undeterred they flew on. As they approached the Channel they met up with a heavy flak barrage from the Calais coastal defences.

The Germans had increased their flak batteries during the war – as they could no longer rely on the Luftwaffe. These powerful 88 millimetre guns could send a 22 pound shell up to a height of 35,000 feet – at a rate of over 15 a minute. If a shell burst within 90 feet of the aircraft, it would be fatal. Inside an area of 600 feet, the shell burst would spray shrapnel and steel splinters about, causing damage to the aircraft and their crews. The German gunners' accuracy at these large B17s flying in formation at a set height and in daylight was deadly.

In less than a minute, *Miss Lollipop* received a hit on number four engine. In the turmoil the waist gunner hollered through the intercom that the engine was on fire. Flak was busting all around them and the shuddering aircraft received another hit on her underbelly, wounding the ball turret gunner. *Miss Lollipop's* number three engine caught alight and the radio operator dragged the gunner to safety and attended to his wounds. The starboard waist gunner screamed to the pilot that the fire was spreading and smoke curled up in the vortex and entered the open bomb bay.

The pilot quickly switched on the fire extinguishers and feathered number three and four propellers. When he saw that it had no effect he put the B17 into a juddering dive, trying to extinguish the flames, but as he levelled up the fire caught again.

By now they were out of the flak field and were almost upon the English coastline. *Miss Lollipop's* number two engine started to sound irregular and became another problem for the stressed pilot to attend to. She was flying at 2,500 feet along the Kent coast with fire and smoke streaming from her wing and the pilot fighting with her controls. This naturally attracted the attention of the Ramsgate and Dover air sea rescue craft that set off in anticipation of the crash which was about to happen. Activated by this emergency, the Walmer lifeboat prepared to launch, her crewmen straining their eyes skywards for parachutes.

The B17's pilot was now having difficulty keeping his ship airborne and ordered his crew to bale out. Below him he could see three minesweepers and he managed to coax the battered plane towards them.

As the hatch door was opened in the waist of the aircraft a rush of smoke-filled air entered. The roar of the flames and struggling engines unnerved the crew. Nevertheless, they knew their lives were hanging by a thread. Their captain shouted at them that he could not hold on for much longer. First to leave was the tail gunner. The port waist gunner watched with horror, as the parachute failed to open and his companion fell silently to his death. As he stood, frozen with fear, the starboard waist gunner took control and pushed him hastily through the opening. Mesmerised, he watched the man hurtle down towards the sea – his parachute also failing to open. Quickly he looked around and, seeing nobody, he leapt from the aperture in the fuselage.

From the front of the plane the engineer made his way to the open bomb bay doors. Out of them he noted the starboard waist gunner floating down under the canopy of his chute and towards the waiting minesweepers. In an instant he dropped through the gaping hole and away from the blazing plane.

Setting the steering of his shaking wreck on to automatic, the pilot was the last man alive to leave. The dying *Miss Lollipop* had dropped to 800 feet when the man baled out and, at such a low height, the pilot's parachute only partially opened before he hit the sea.

At a quarter past nine on that June morning *Miss Lollipop* dived into the sea off St Margaret's Bay, south of Deal. Aluminium was stripped away from her flak-splattered body and the weight of her engines quickened her descent in 60 feet of water. The flames were extinguished, and only a layer of aviation fuel settled on the surface to display where this fighting machine had once been.

Walmer lifeboat had launched at twenty minutes past nine, after the pilot had been seen baling out of his flaming aircraft. When the crew found him two-and-a-half miles south of their station, the westerly wind had just enough strength to make some chop on the sea. The pilot's condition was serious, and the coxswain of the *Charles Dibden Civil Service No 4* lifeboat immediately headed back to shore. Once the poor man had been taken from them they returned to search for any other survivors. The brave pilot, Lt McKeague, was later to die of his injuries.

Searching east of the Goodwin Sands, a minesweeper picked up the starboard waist gunner and the engineer from the choppy sea, 25 minutes after they had landed. The air-sea rescue craft steered an easterly course from the crash area towards the minesweepers and came across the dead body of the aircraft's bombardier. The rest of *Miss Lollipop's* crew were listed as 'missing in action'.

In the midst of the D-Day landings, this tragic incident was soon forgotten. They were part of the 'big push' – part of the 800 American airmen from the 'Bloody Hundredths' and 8th Air Force who forfeited their lives to bring peace to Europe.

The summer of 1995, Bob Peacock and a group of divers from *Sea Dive* discovered the B17's remains. They saw the rotting remnants of the aluminium fuselage and airframe, four large radial engines and their propellers. As they had found live ammunition on the wreck they informed the relevant authorities.

Shortly after, a group of navy divers, from Southern Diving Unit 2, recovered 0.5 calibre bullets and a Browning machine gun from the aircraft. As a mark of respect they left the rest undisturbed and laid a wreath on the wreckage of this poignant war grave.

Walmer lifeboat saved the pilot, however, he later died from his wounds.

This Wellington carried an extra crewman

SECRET MISSION

Wellington bomber DV-819 taxied down the concrete runway at RAF Gransden Lodge in Bedfordshire. The time was two in the morning, the date was 3rd December 1942, and its mission was secret.

Pilot Ted Paulton checked with the navigator, Bill Barry, on both the compass course and an estimated time of arrival. The radio operator, Bill Bigoray, cleared it with the airfield's control tower that everything was functional and they were awaiting clearance for take-off.

RAF Gransden Lodge was set in a secluded location, which was ideal for its secret activities. There were three runways with a maximum length of 2,000 yards and in the hangers and sidings there stood other Wellingtons, Halifaxes, Mosquitoes and Anson bombers. This station was number 1474 Flight and its role was 'Enemy Signal Investigation'.

The Wellington DV-819's mission was to try and discover the radar frequency that the German night fighters were using with so much success. Alongside the radio operator was an extra crewman, Harold Jordan. He was a special operator and the only Englishman amongst the Canadian volunteer aircrew. His electronic equipment, capable of probing the enemy fighter plane's radar, took up most of the aircraft's bulkhead. The Wellington and her crew had, in the past, been on 17 lone sorties – but none of them had tempted a night fighter to appear. The Luftwaffe knew that British technology was capable of finding the frequency of their Lichtenstein C-1 radar, and were much too suspicious to rise to the RAF's bait.

This time it was decided to use a new tact. DV-819's destination was to meet up with another 112 bombers which were on a raid to Frankfurt. She would not hold any bombs as an extra 250 gallon fuel tank was inserted in her bomb bay. Their plan was to act as a straggler, hoping that the Germans would not realise they were a decoy.

As the Wellington droned over the Channel, Everett Vachon asked his skipper if he could test his guns. He was the aeroplane's rear gunner and youngest of the team at 22 years of age. With an affirmative from the pilot officer, he let a quick burst fly from his four ·303

Browning machine guns. This was quickly followed by another burst from the forward gunner, Fred Grant.

DV-819 contacted the main force of Allied bombers and tagged on to the rear of the flight. Just before they reached Frankfurt, their plan was to drop away from the other aircraft and fly north, acting as if she had lost her way from the main flight.

Before this could happen, Jordan started to pick up radiation on his radar screen. He quickly tuned it into the pulses and found that the unknown stalker was using 492 megacycles. He asked the radio operator to broadcast a coded message of his findings back to base. Bigoray logged the time, 4.30am, and tapped out the information. Within seconds, he received conformation of his message from RAF Gransden Lodge.

The pulses were getting stronger and they decided to dangle a little more bait. Paulton swung the Wellington to the north and away from the other bombers. This manoeuvre would not only confirm that it was the enemy, but also be a chance to make sure that they had the right frequency. Knowing that they were tempting an unremitting onslaught, the bravery of these men was to be admired. If their aircraft was destroyed and they were lucky enough to bail out and then be captured, they would be shot as spies.

Within minutes, Jordan, glued to his electronics, saw that the signals were pulsating on his receiver at full strength. Out of the blackness a JU88 night fighter attached herself to the Wellington's tail.

Everett Vachon hardly had time to adjust his hydraulically operated rear gun turret, as cannon shells hurtled towards him. He was now wishing that he was back home and working on the farm in Québec rather than have to face this nightmare. Before he could site up on the twin-engine fighter, Paulton put the DV-819 into an evasive dive.

The initial cannon shells that the JU88 had fired had already done some damage. Jordan had received a hit in his left arm and holes had appeared in the fuselage from the 20 millimetre cannon shells. The special operator was in pain, however he had confirmed the enemy's radar frequency and yet again asked for Bigoray to send it out and wait for a reply. This was done – but this time there was no incoming response.

The screen in front of Jordan came to life again. He warned the crew that they were in for another onslaught. The rear gunner tensed himself, peering through the blackness. Tracers from the 20 millimetre cannon shells sped towards him before he could even see the German night-fighter. The JU88's cannon had far greater range than Vachon's Browning · 303s.

Armour-piecing shells tore into the Wellington, wounding the gunner and rendering the hydraulics of his turret useless. By twirling the aerials, Jordan could see which direction the JU88 was going to approach from next. He shouted a warning to the forward gunner that the enemy was coming in fast from that direction. Again, the night-fighter let rip with her cannon and 7·9 millimetre machine guns. Regardless of this, Fred Grant managed to get a burst off from his Brownings before the German's bullets ripped into his turret putting a hole in his right leg. As Bigoray helped Grant he also received a wound.

The Wellington bomber was at the JU88's mercy. More bullets sprayed the aircraft and again the radio operator, Harold Jordan, felt another one hit him, this time in the jaw.

The crew were relying on the pilot. Paulton and the navigator were the only other persons aboard who were unhurt. The pilot had his engines running at maximum revolutions but he knew that his speed was no match against the 300 mph of his enemy.

From under its radar antenna, once more the German's guns spat out their deadly torrent. Again, the men received more wounds and blood was flowing over their leather flying jackets on to their boots.

Through this carnage, the radio operator was continuing to send the Morse message to base, yet was still not getting a reply.

Ted Paulton dropped the Wellington from a height of 13,000 feet to a mere 500 feet off the ground. He was doing everything in his power to lose the persistent German. For the crew, awaiting Jordan's warning of another attack, it seemed a lifetime. Five minutes went by, then ten. Jordan informed them that his electronics showed no signs of the other aircraft's radar signals. They gratefully concluded that the JU88 had run out of ammunition.

Men aboard DV-819 breathed a sigh of relief. They tended to each others' wounds the best they could and checked out the damage.

The German's shells had caused chaos. The half-inch armour plate at the back of Paulton's seat was the only thing that had saved him. However, the starboard aileron had been shot off, his starboard engine throttle destroyed and the engines were racing out of control. The pilot fought to keep the Wellington on a course the navigator had given him for England. This had been a difficult task as Barry's chart was now covered in Jordan's blood. Eventually he got the battered plane to a height of 5,000 feet, levelled off and flew over the French coast towards Britain.

Two hours had gone by since their attack. The Wellington's engines were red hot, yet still they kept going. As Paulton headed for the Kent coast, he knew the aircraft would not be capable of a normal landing.

Amongst the crew there was confusion that their message of the radar frequencies had not been received. They could not accept that they had been through this ordeal without a reason. It was decided that one of them should bail out with the information secured upon their person.

As they made the Kent coast, it was to be Bill Bigoray who squeezed through the escape hatch in the belly of the aeroplane. The rest of the crew watched as his parachute billowed in the dawn light. Miraculously, he landed in the grounds of Ramsgate Hospital.

The pilot, Ted Paulton, coaxed the bomber down to sea level. Smoke was coming from the over-heated engines. He had realised that, if he could pancake his aircraft on the sea successfully, they would only have a few minutes before she sank.

As the aircrew braced themselves, they could hardly believe their luck when Paulton delivered the manoeuvre effectively. A small local fishing boat was on the scene in minutes and relieved the sinking aircraft of her crew. All this had happened only a few hundred yards offshore from the village of Kingsdown, near Deal.

The acquisition of the Luftwaffe's radar frequencies helped the Allies for a few months, but swift alterations were made when the enemy realised what had happened.

In the winter of 1955, a dinghy coming ashore from the 'Deal & Walmer Angling Association's Boat Fishing Festival' suddenly came to an abrupt halt. Being low water, one of the blades of DV-819's propeller had pierced the wooden dinghy throwing the four occupants into the sea. Other boats in the fishing competition soon rendered assistance.

The following week, on the instruction of the Air Ministry, the engine was removed from the sea and dumped on to the beach. What became of this famous piece of World War Two memorabilia is unknown.

Part of an aircraft's landing gear

Heavy seas pound the *Luray Victory*

VICTORY ON THE SANDS

Throughout the winter of 1945, it was a common sight to see the large American *Liberty* and *Victory* ships in and around the sea-ways of the English Channel. The war had just ended with the defeat of the Nazis and, although Britain was on rationing, it was Europe which was starving and desperate for food. These 7,612 ton *Victory* ships would be full of supplies from the vast American nation – which had been least effected by the devastation of the past war.

Although there were great similarities between the *Victory* and the *Liberty* ships, the *Victory* was slightly larger with outsized cargo booms and more efficient winches. They also had a faster turn of speed – although designed for 15½ knots, the engineers could push the turbines to attain 17 knots. Aptly named, the *Victorys* were mass-produced, with 200 a year being built from 19 American shipyards during 1944.

From Baltimore, bound for Bremerhaven, the *Luray Victory* had been at maximum speed in the Atlantic, and as she approached the Straits of Dover, she did not decrease. The evening of January 30th 1946, the ship was thundering up the Channel towards the Goodwin Sands. She had no pilot aboard, as the American War Shipping Administration had advised the masters that there was no need of them. According to them, the English Channel was 'relatively free of dangers'.

The west-north-west wind had the makings of a Channel gale and darkness was made darker by the rolling masses of cloud that hid the stars. On approaching the south-eastern corner of the Goodwins, the *Luray Victory* lost the deep water and, without warning, ran up on to the sandbank. The jolt and the abrupt way at which she came to a halt immobilised her engine.

At nine o'clock that night, the *Luray Victory's* chief engineer declared that he was at a loss to repair the machinery and the captain, through a radio transmission, summoned the advice of the coast guard.

When the North Deal coast guard station fired the maroons, the *Charles Dibden* lifeboat was just coming ashore. They had been out on an earlier shout and had spent three hours searching the Goodwin Sands for a large Liberty ship, *Am-Mer-Mar*. Her captain had reported that she was stranded, however, the ship had managed to dislodge herself unaided, and the lifeboat had been ordered to return to Walmer beach.

Freddie Upton had been coxswain of the *Charles Dibden* for only seven months but his local knowledge and seamanship was paramount in the area. He questioned those ashore if there had been some confusion between the present distress summons and the previous one. Being assured this was a fresh casualty, they turned the lifeboat around on the turn table and re-launched into the darkness.

Coxswain Upton found the *Luray Victory* at twenty-seven minutes past ten that night. The ship was aground on the Sands and seas were breaking around her. With the aid of a signal lamp, Upton conveyed that it was too dangerous to go along side, but they instead would lay-off and await dawn. In the early hours some tugs arrived, and at six in the morning the lifeboat up-anchored and helped transfer their wire hawsers to the stranded victim. Every effort to re-float the *Luray Victory* at high water failed and the ship took on a list to port.

Although the American captain requested the lifeboat to continually stand-by his vessel, Freddie Upton refused. He knew she was in no immediate danger and, being low on fuel, motored back to the lifeboat house. The *Charles Dibden* had been afloat since seven twenty-eight the previous evening – apart from the thirty minutes she had beached and returned to sea – and his men were tired and hungry.

Coxswain Upton speculated that they would have to spend another night with the casualty and bade his men to put some dry clothes on and get a quick meal. This they did and within two hours the *Charles Dibden* was back at sea. By this time the wind had backed to the south, and it was still blowing gale force. It was an uncomfortable journey. They had to motor the long way around the Sands, via the *South Goodwin* lightship, to reach the outside edge.

As the lifeboat hove in sight, an hour later, at four o'clock on that grey afternoon, Upton could see that the ship was starting to break up. The tugs had stood well away as their services were futile. They only remained there as witnesses to this ship's demise. The wreck's list had been exaggerated and spray was cascading up and over the weather side of the hull drenching the deserted decks.

Walmer lifeboat *Charles Dibden* visits the wreck

The captain of the *Luray Victory* signalled, by Aldis lamp, that he was going to abandon ship. He and his crew had felt their ship being destroyed by the weather and the Goodwins. Their large steel haven in which they had put all their trust was fast becoming a monstrous tomb. The hull was making awful groaning noises as the welds split and then loud cracks as gaping gashes appeared. Dark, sandy sea water was entering her holds, spoiling the cargo of grain.

The stranded hulk had her lifeboats swung out on her davits and men were seen to be getting ready to board them. Upton knew that to do this would have been suicidal. With the falling tide, the ships keel at the stern was starting to show. The tide was sluicing along the hull with confused waves beating against it. Upton ordered double the amount of fenders to be tied from the bow to amidships of the *Charles Dibden*. With the help of his motor mechanic, Percy Cavell, he approached the towering hull.

Freddie's voice became hoarse with constant instructions to Percy on how he wanted the control of his engines. As he nudged the lifeboat closer, his crew started to prepare themselves for the unknown. It took immense skill to con the craft alongside, where a Jacob's ladder had been hung from the ship's side. Eagerly awaiting and clinging to each rung of the ladder, was a crewman from the American vessel.

The coxswain on the helm, was fighting with the wheel. There were cross seas sweeping against the ship's side that were trying to push the lifeboat away — despite this he still managed to keep contact. With the small boat's engines going in and out of gear the *Charles Dibden* continued to bump against the welded hull. Each time the two vessels came together another sailor jumped into the sturdy craft. Miraculously, the entire crew of 49 made the transaction without injury.

With all of the grateful men in the lifeboat her hull lay deep in the swirling waves. Freddie Upton steered his craft south, into the teeth of the gale, to make another rounding of the *South Goodwin* lightship. The heavily-laden craft disappeared at times in the enormous waves and it was not until she turned to the north-west and home that she had the weather and seas on her port quarter.

The boat came safely ashore in a flurry of spray and the men, with the effects of adrenalin wearing off, felt cold and weary. None of the *Luray Victory's* sailors had time to thank the lifeboat men, as they were whisked off by the Lloyds Agent and the American Authorities to warmer accommodation.

Later Freddie Upton reflected on the rescue, and in his report he wrote… 'The coxswain wishes to record his appreciation of the splendidly efficient manner in which his crew carried through this very arduous service. The number of survivors brought ashore at one time is believed to be a record. The American crew was mixed – white and coloured. The job of getting them in the lifeboat, which involved them jumping from considerable height was extremely hazardous. Altogether a fine service.'

It did not take long for the *Luray Victory* to completely split in half and she did so just forward of the bridge. The bow section was swept a few hundred feet away and was quickly overwhelmed by the Goodwins. Some salvage was attempted on the other half and a couple of hundred tons of cereals were removed, but the rest of the waterlogged grain was left.

The sand bank did its best to swallow the remaining stern half of ship and succeeded until the wreck found the Goodwins chalk subsurface. When the upright hull sat upon the foundations of the Goodwin Sands, only the king posts still showed. This spectacle has remained until the present day and is the only visual reminder of the menace which lies six miles off – although the American War Shipping Administration deemed the area as 'relatively free of dangers'.

To predict the Sand's movements are almost impossible – it can cover as well as expose wreckage on a tide. In the summer of 1991, Barry Curtis, a Medway scuba diver, found an 18 inch high by 18 inch wide bell on the remains of the wreck. This massive bronze item weighed 78 pounds and, sadly as expected for a mass-produced Victory ship, it did not have her name inscribed upon it.

The *Nancy Moran* was on loan from the United States War Shipping Administration

DEADLY FOG

The circumstances were similar to the sinking of the *Peter Hawksfield,* but the outcome was deadlier. In the early hours of Thursday 30ᵗʰ May 1946, thick fog had once more engulfed the Goodwin Sands and the Downs. Ships not wanting to risk collision had anchored up. The sounds of gongs, bells and horns reverberated throughout the vicinity – hopefully making aware their position to those foolhardy enough to still be navigating through the Straits of Dover.

Captain Arthur Harris, a Kent man from Folkestone, was the skipper of the tug *Nancy Moran.* He was 45 years old and had spent much of his working life on the pilot cutters. This experience had given him the knowledge of knowing his way around the coast between England and France.

The tug was on loan from the United States War Shipping Administration to the British Ministry of Transport. The English Channel would have been a far cry from the Pacific coastline that the tug had been used to working from. However, she was a big and powerful vessel and was being useful, in a small way, to assist in getting Britain back on her feet after an arduous war.

Nancy Moran had secured the towing of a large mud-hopper, *Titan 2*, from Southampton to London. Night, along with the thick fog, had made it impossible to navigate through the confined waters in the approach to the Thames Estuary. Captain Harris knew he was in the vicinity of the Goodwin Sands and reluctantly anchored up.

As darkness fell, the fog shrouded the vessel in a spectral gloom. After supper, most of the 19 crew settled down for the night. With such a large complement of men onboard, it gave the majority of them the chance of a good night's sleep – which would not be interfered with by having to stand a watch. The captain, hoping the fog would soon lift, displayed the relevant lights to indicate that the vessels were at anchor. He knew that the lights were only a token in the thick fog. Close to the east, he could hear the deep cow-like bellow of the *South Goodwin* lightship. The horn was discharging its high and low pitch moan, twice every minute.

It was not known why the oil tanker *Nuculana* was navigating so close to the Goodwin Sands, however, at four in the morning and without warning she almost cut the *Nancy*

Moran in half. The men on watch had no time to shout out warnings as the tanker loomed out of the fog. In an instant, everybody was awakened with the sound of crashing, tearing steel. Men were thrown out of their bunks as the *Nancy Moran* lurched and nearly folded in half. The force of the collision parted the tow rope from the mud-hopper. In less than three minutes, the tug had sunk and the men were floundering in the dark sea.

The *Nuculana* stopped her engines and launched two motorized lifeboats to search for the missing tug's crew.

Two of the *Nancy Moran's* crewmen had managed to swim to the mud-hopper and scramble aboard. With their wet clothes sticking to their bodies, they tried to launch the rowing boat which was chocked up on its deck. Amid the shouts for help from the floundering men in the water, the two men made a frenzied final effort to dislodge the boat from its chocks. Breathlessly they had to give up. The boat was too heavy and they were too exhausted. By this time the wind was blowing the mud-hopper along a little faster than the tide. Frantically, the two men aboard her threw ropes and planks of wood in the direction of their slowly vanishing friends. The men in the water were trying their best to keep up – but were tiring fast. They thankfully clung on the jettisoned timber, as the hopper drifted out of sight in the fog.

An hour later, the *Nuculana's* motor boats found some of the men in the midst of the oil and debris that was floating on the surface. Although it was nearly June, the sea was still cold and the struggling men were recovered with haste. They also rescued the two men off the mud-hopper. Several hours went by and they continued the search. After a head count, it was discovered that six men were still unaccounted for – Captain Harris was one of them.

Nearby, crewmen on the *South Goodwin* lightship heard men crying out from the sea. They radioed ashore and notified the coastguard station and the Walmer lifeboat was launched.

When the *Nuculana's* lifeboats came upon the lightship, the rescued men were relocated on to her.

Within the hour the Walmer lifeboat, *Charles Dibden*, moored up alongside the lightship and the shipwrecked men were transferred on to her. Two of the men needed urgent medical attention and, fortunately, the lifeboat's doctor, James Hall, was aboard to tend to the tugs crew. Doctor Hall felt that the men needed to be taken ashore for treatment and the lifeboat returned to Walmer.

Promptly, the *Charles Dibden* was re-launched and, just after eight in the morning, revisited the wreck site to look for the missing men. The mist had lifted but they could not find any more survivors. They did come across the mud-hopper, *Titan 2*, drifting two miles from the *South Goodwin* light vessel. They searched the vessel further, hoping to find the lost seamen, but found that their hunt was fruitless and the hopper's deck was empty. The tug *Lady Brassey* secured the derelict vessel and towed it back to Dover.

Relentlessly the lifeboat crew investigated any surface flotsam that they spied. By noon, reluctantly, the search was called off – no more men or bodies had been found. When the *Charles Dibden* hit the beach on her return, the previous 13 crewmen from the *Nancy Moran* surrounded the craft, frantically peering over her gunnels. The sombre faces of the lifeboat crew told them the story of no hope, however one of them still asked the coxswain if he had found his brother. The solemn answer given was 'No luck…'

There were no words, no description for their profound misery.

Fog might deaden man's senses but not his feelings. Telegrams were sent to inform the relatives of the missing *Nancy Moran's* crewmembers and sadness was felt by many families in Kent and Essex.

Eventually, the invention of radar helped to solve the problems of navigation through the natural phenomenon of fog – but the fear of it is still installed in every mariner who sails on every sea.

A tangle of masts that were to last almost 50 years

CHRISTMAS ON THE GOODWINS

Sadly missed are the group of masts from a wreck that graced the skyline off Deal for 49 years. Almost five miles offshore, on the Goodwin Sands, were the remains and the masts of a 7,612 ton American vessel. Although they were precariously angled, they were always visible at all states of the tide. They stood 30 feet high, with one of the mast's crosstrees looking like a monumental crucifix. One by one, they were slowly removed by winter gales until the last single remaining mast disappeared, almost unnoticed, in the last weeks of January 1995. Taken for granted all of those years, they were always a welcoming sight to the Deal boatmen – to view them looming out of the mist gave them their position instantly in an otherwise fogbound surround.

It was fog that was the cause of the wrecking of the Lyke Line's *North Eastern Victory*. She was steaming up the Channel at the maximum speed that her 6,000 horse power engine could propel her. The captain wanted to spend Christmas day in Antwerp and, as it was on the morning of Christmas Eve 1946, he was pulling out all of the stops to attain his goal. Unbeknown to him, a spring tide was increasing his speed by an extra four knots, and he sped through the Straits of Dover at 21 knots. As he passed the *South Goodwin* lightship he did not notice, or perhaps ignored, that the light-float was firing a cannon to summon his attention.

The American War Administration had cautioned the *Victory's* captains against taking on pilots in this part of the coastline, deeming it unnecessary. According to them there were few dangers lurking in the Straits of Dover or the North Sea. They also issued charts without the details of the light vessels and buoys which surrounded one of the most dangerous sandbanks in the world, the Goodwin Sands. The *South, East* and *North Goodwin* lightships had only just been replaced on station after the battering they had endured during the war. It would be the crews on these vessels that had seen the most cavalier actions taken by the *Liberty* and *Victory* ships' captains in and around the Sands. In the past 12 months, there had been two total ship losses and many near escapes – all of them American.

The compass gimbal found on the wreck

With the warning gun of the lightship going unheeded, it was to be the Deal boatmen who would need to get prepared for any events that were about to happen. These shots were aimed as a forewarning to the *North Eastern Victory* that she was steaming too close to the Goodwins. The ship's speed of 21 knots soon carried them past the light vessel as it disappeared into the fog.

The whole ship juddered to a halt as she ran up in the shallow water onto the sandbank near the *East Goodwin* Lightship. Not only did the impact smash most of the ship's crockery but it also carried away her wireless aerials. The 440 feet welded steel hull lay motionless, completely and helplessly stranded. No distress call could be made on the wireless equipment and, with the fog engulfing her, it would have been pointless to have set off flares or rockets.

The ex-coxswain of the Walmer lifeboat, Joe Mercer, was close to 70, although his years did not stop him going afloat. At the sound of the *South Goodwin* light vessel firing her guns, he knew there might be a chance of a bit of work to be had. In the Deal motor boat, *Rose Marie,* he set a compass course of east-south-east through the fog and towards a part of the Goodwins they had nicknamed 'Calamity Corner'. He was not to be disappointed as he and his two crewmen came across the slab-sided ship almost high and dry.

With the dexterity of a man half his age, he climbed up the rope and wooden slatted ladder that had been offered. He went and looked forward, aft then amidships of the vessel, shaking his head continuously. In conversation with the *North Eastern Victory's* skipper, Captain Kohstrohs, he stated that the ship had little water around her and even less amidships. This would mean that the ship would soon break her back. Within minutes of this pronouncement the chief engineer entered the bridge and reported to the captain that there were splits in the hull and the engine room was becoming flooded. This gave credibility to Mercer's statement and the captain became pensive for a while.

Kohstrohs had not counted on this delay – he had 5000 tons of flour, 1000 tons of rice, 10,000 cases of grapefruit, plus cotton and lead in his holds, which had to be offloaded at Antwerp, Rotterdam and Bremen. He conferred with Mercer as to what course of action he should take. The answer was not what he had wished for. The ex-lifeboat coxswain declared he felt that there was no chance for the ship, and recommended that his main concern should be for the welfare of his crew. The captain begrudgingly accepted his predicament and asked the Deal boatman to summon the lifeboat. Before Joe Mercer left the stranded vessel, Captain Kohstrohs offered him a leg of turkey that the cook had been preparing. With a good hearted retort, the old boatman proclaimed he would sooner have a piece of the prime cut off the breast, than a leg, and left the ship for the last time.

Late that afternoon, he got ashore and reported the circumstances to the lifeboat coxswain, Freddie Upton. At five minutes past five that afternoon, the *Charles Dibden* launched into an unruffled sea.

With the sea being calm the rescue was a simple one. Thirty-six of the crew were transferred into the lifeboat without difficulty. The captain and his six officers decided that they would remain aboard the stranded vessel and await and see what salvage efforts could be made. As Upton left, he noted that the ship was almost completely broken in half with her side split and a two-foot gash through her deck. By 10 o'clock that night, he had offloaded his human cargo, refuelled and was back on station alongside the *North Eastern Victory*.

The vigil was to become a night of adversity in the freezing conditions. Their only relief was the cold turkey that the ship's crew had abandoned and few tots of rum. Dawn on Christmas day was greeted with a blood-red sunrise – a sure sign that there was bad weather coming. Through the *Charles Dibden's* wireless, the coastguard alerted coxswain Upton that a gale was already sweeping up the Channel. Even the lifeboat was restlessly surging against her mooring ropes that tethered her alongside the ship. The men knew it was time to leave. The ship was making noises unnatural to their ears — sounds of groaning, creaking and cracking. The rent which had appeared immediately forward of the bridge and down the hull was   noticeably opening up and the vessel took on a list.

Freddie Upton convinced the officers that there was nothing more to be done and with a look of shock they left their ship that was less than a year and a half old. As they boarded the *Charles Dibden* one of the ships officers commented that a rusty shipwreck half a mile away, on the same sand bank, had a similar outline to their own *Victory* ship. Upton merely nodded; he knew it would only be a matter of time before this ship became the equivalent to the nearby wreck of the *Luray Victory*. The lifeboat raced for home and the crew spent what was left of Christmas Day with their families.

Days went by and the familiar characteristic peculiarity of the bow leaving the rest of the welded ship's hull quickly happened. It was swept 100 feet away and disappeared into the sand. From the remaining non-submerged part of the ship the cargo was salvaged, in-between gales, by Risdon Beazley Ltd. Strangely, at that time, the ration restricted households of Deal seemed to have a plentiful supply of tins of grapefruit – origin on the tins, New Orleans, the port of departure of the *North Eastern Victory*.

Shortly after, the American War Administration board revised their orders to the captains about not taking pilots – and also revised the charts. They now issued ones that marked the Goodwin Sands as a danger; however, it was only a matter of three months later before another of their ships was lost on Calamity Corner, a few hundred yards away from the others.

The weakness of these mass-produced ships was in their welded hull, nevertheless many survived and sailed the oceans of the world for years. Even the masts of the *North Eastern Victory* endured the Channel gales for almost half a century – until they disappeared for ever and became sadly missed by the local populace.

North Eastern Victory nearing her end

Silvia Onorato's back is already broken

HAPPY BIRTHDAY FREDDIE

The coxswain, Freddie Upton, and his crew of the Walmer Lifeboat *Charles Dibden Civil Service No 2* justifiably had a pride in their craft. This was to be the first motor lifeboat at Walmer. She had cost £7,000, a vast sum in the 1930s, and was 41 feet long. Only skilled shipwrights were used in the building of the 16 ton vessel and she had been specially designed for beach use. The keel was made of the finest teak with the stem and stern post from English oak and she was double planked with Honduras mahogany fixed to Canadian Rock elm timbers. There were two 35hp engines, which gave her a speed of nearly eight knots. In the hull over 130 air cases were secured and with her relieving scuppers, which could cope with any amount of water on deck, she was totally unsinkable. The *Charles Dibden* would carry a crew of 10, and, at a pinch, squeeze another 76 people on board in an emergency. Paint and varnish on the boat were clean and the crew always made sure the brass fittings were bright and shiny.

However, there were times when she was launched and Freddie Upton was not at the helm. One such day was on the 2nd January 1948.

It was at the start of the sprat season and many of the boatmen were taking advantage of a break in the winter weather – although a cold wet breeze had produced a damp mist, or what the Deal men would call 'clag'. The wind had freshened, clearing the fog, and it was driving Freddie's sprat nets along with the tide.

Within nine minutes of the time of the maroons being fired from the Deal coastguard station, the lifeboat had been launched. Her temporary skipper had steamed the *Charles Dibden* towards the small boat from which Freddie had his nets strung. After having a quick word to his mate, Freddie Upton left him in charge to haul the nets. He then boarded the lifeboat.

He was hastily told the cause for the launch. When the fog had lifted the coastguard officer had spied a ship aground in the middle of the Goodwin Sands.

The wind was getting stronger by the minute and the sky was overcast with a drizzling rain. Visibility was about a mile and it was at that distance when they sighted the ship.

Aground on a falling tide was the *Silvia Onorato* of 2,327 tons. She was an Italian ship registered in Naples, which had come from Rijecka, in the Adriatic, and was bound for Rotterdam. When Upton took the lifeboat over the Sands, he found the seas were confused and unpredictable. Different wind directions over the shoal waters of the Goodwins produces wave actions that cannot always be comprehended. The sea on this day looked as if it was boiling.

As he approached the *Silvia Onorato* a wave, larger than the rest, lifted the lifeboat on the top of its crest. He and his crew looked down on the cargo hatches of the stranded ship as they were swept towards her. Before the *Charles Dibden* hit, the wave subsided and grazed the little craft against the ship's hull. It was a test for the sturdiness of the lifeboat which was a credit to her shipwrights.

Cautiously, Freddie went alongside again and a crewman jumped onto the Jacob's ladder that was offered. Once aboard he had difficulty in conversing with the ships master, Captain Francesco Ruocco. The Italian skipper was brown-faced with bushy black eye-brows. His knowledge of the English language was monosyllabic and the Deal lifeboat man's Kentish dialect did not help the situation. Ruocco's only concern was to get off the sandbank and continue his journey. The lifeboat man explained that if he could use full power and steam himself off the bank he would be in deeper water.

It was a ruse that Ruocco was prepared to try, and as his chief engineer produced all the steam he could — the vibrating ship moved forward. The whole exercise was futile, because as she cleared one bank she went hard up onto the next in the falling tide. Under her there was only 14 feet of water, and the *Silvia Onorato* drew 18 feet at the bows and 20 feet aft.

The *Charles Dibden* was standing-by, off the ship's port side, however, the weather was getting worse and Upton did not want to stay that close for the low water. As he went alongside to pick up his crewman, the coxswain offered to take the rest of the Italian ship's men as well. His answer was given in broken English 'My ship, my life. Ship go, me go.' Freddie Upton hailed the captain that the lifeboat would have to stand-by at anchor in deeper water – and, if he was required urgently, send up a rocket. It was to be a cold and uncomfortable night and the lifeboat's meagre ration of rum and biscuits were soon used up.

Before dawn arrived, Upton had up-anchored and was in attendance around the stranded vessel while the tide made. After another futile attempt to extricate herself, the Italian stopped his engine from going ahead. Upton put the lifeboat as close as possible and shouted out that he had to go ashore to refuel, but would be back as soon as possible. This was done within an hour and the *Charles Dibden* was again motoring back out to the Goodwins before nine o'clock that morning.

Around this time the 'clag' was starting to descend and, as they approached her, the lifeboat men lost sight of the *Silvia Onorato* on more than one occasion. Nevertheless, the 'clag' had heralded the wind – which soon dispersed the mist. Before darkness descended for the second night it was blowing a gale with heavy seas running.

Daybreak on Sunday 4th January was Freddie Upton's 51st birthday. He would have preferred to have celebrated it ashore, however he had a job that needed doing. He weighed anchor yet again and conned the lifeboat through the rough sea towards the ship. Again the captain refused the offer to rescue his crew. He stated that his vessel was still sound and he and his crew were happy to stay aboard.

Upton made the journey back across the broken water on the Goodwins towards the lifeboat station. He beached at nine that morning to refuel, get a bite to eat and a change of clothes. The tired men gratefully ate Sunday dinner and had a nap before they were back afloat at three and along side the *Silvia Onorato* by twenty-past four in the afternoon.

This time Freddie Upton went aboard the ship to try and convince her captain that there would be no saving of his vessel. As he climbed the ladder and stuck his head above the ship's side, he was confronted by the large head of an Alsatian dog. Upton had braved many tremendous seas and had courageously and daringly undertaken numerous rescues – but this was the most terrifying moment of his career.

After the dog had licked Freddie's face, the captain, in Italian, called it to heel. It was to be a very well-behaved and docile animal.

The lifeboat coxswain explained all the dangers of staying and tried to convince Captain Ruocco that it was pointless to remain. Again he said 'Ship go, me go'. The Italian was adamant and Upton left the ship disappointed. The lifeboat started to leave the vessel for another night at anchor when a radio message, from Lloyds Shipping Agents, alerted them to a severe weather warning. There was going to be a severe gale, force nine and imminent from the south-south-west, with winds gusting up to fifty knots.

Charles Dibden was turned about and went alongside the ship once more. With the aid of a loud hailer the lifeboat coxswain relayed the bad weather forecast. This time Upton would not take no for an answer. With the lifeboat alongside, the 28 crew disembarked from their doomed ship. Almost the last to leave would have been Captain Francesco Ruocco and his Alsatian dog; however, two stowaways emerged from their hiding place. These were to be two Germans who had secretly boarded the *Silvia Onorato* when she had left the Adriatic and were looking for a better future after the war.

The ride back to the lifeboat station was perilous. More than once Freddie had to slam the *Charles Dibden* out of gear as she rose onto a big wave that crested in front of the bow. Fifty-five minutes later, they reached the shore and the beach-crew pulled the lifeboat, with its rescued sailors, up onto its turntable.

In two days, the *Silvia Onorato's* back broke, between the bridge and funnel. The fore part of the ship listed to starboard and the stern section stayed bolt upright. The captain was taken out to this part of the wreck, for the last time, to pick up the crew's personal possessions – which comprised mainly wine and cigarettes. As he said his silent goodbye to his beloved ship, he wondered why no tugs had been present to help. Perhaps the answer to that quandary was possibly that the ship was 32 years old and in the past had been mined, sunk and refloated after being submerged for four years. She also had a low value cargo.

Although Francesco Ruocco clearly loved his ship, apparently it was worthless rusting metal to others. Either way, it was the Goodwin Sands that finally possessed her and embraced her in its clutches – never to be seen again.

Silvia Onorato before the Goodwins 'swaddled' her

APPENDIX

Position of the **_ROOSWIJK_**   51°- 16′- ? N.   01°- 34′- ? E
Dutch East Indiaman. Built in 1737 at Amsterdam. Length 150 feet, Beam 50 feet. 850 tons.
At time of loss owned by the Verenigde Oostindische Compagnie (VOC).

Position of the **_LOANDA_**   51°- 08′- 96N.   01°- 24′- 70E.
Steamship. Built in 1891 by Naval Construction & Armaments Co, Barrow. Length 327 feet.
Beam 39 feet. 2702 GRT. At time of loss owned by Elder Dempster line.

Position of the **_FLORES_**   51°- 12′- 91N.   01°- 24′- 22E.
Schooner. Built in 1890 in Brazil. 47 tons. Nothing else known.

Position of the **_ARIES_**   51°- 08′-10N.   01°- 23′- 80E.
Steam yacht. Built in 1881 at Barrow. Length 145 feet. Beam 20 feet. 201 GRT. At time of
loss owned by the Duke of Leeds.

Position of the **_ETOILE POLAIRE_**   51°- 09′- 10N.   01°- 28′- 18E.
Armed steam trawler. Built in 1914 by J.T.Eltringham Co Ltd, Newcastle. Length 142 feet.
Beam 23 feet. 278 GRT. At time of loss owned by the Admiralty.

Position of the **_DE LA POLE_**   51°- 11′- 63N.   01°- 32′- 87E.
Requisitioned steam trawler. Built in 1911 by Cook, Welton and Gemmell Ltd, Beverly.
Length 121 feet. Beam 23 feet. 255 GRT. At time of loss owned by the Admiralty.

Position of the **_PIAVE_**   51°- 15′- 17N.   01°- 30′- 34E.
Steam ship. Built in 1918 by Fedral Ship Building Co, Kearny. Length 396 feet. Beam 55
feet. 6,869 GRT. At time of loss owned by United States Shipping Board.

Position of the **_TOOGO_**   51°- 15′- 20N.   01°- 27′- 42E.
Three masted schooner. Built in 1907 by J.Lauri, Kertel. Length 91 feet. Beam 26 feet. 157
GRT. At time of loss owned by J and T. Woleus.

Position of the **_CORINTHIAN_**   51°- 16′- 20N.   01°- 29′- 90E.
Ketch barge. Built in 1892 by Beeching, Yarmouth. Length 98 feet. Beam 21 feet. 94 GRT.
At time of loss owned by Garnham and Chelmondiston

Position of the **_FALCON_**   51°- 07′- 88N.   01°- 21′- 14E.
Steamship. Built in 1876 by C.Mitchell & Co, Newcastle. Length 200 feet. Beam 27 feet.
675 GRT. At time of loss owned by General Steam Navigation Co.

Position of the *PETER HAWKSFIELD*   51°- 11′- 19N.   01°- 25′- 90E.
Steam ship. Built in 1918 by Dundee Ship Building Co, Glasgow. Length 200 feet. Beam 32 feet. 959 GRT. At time of loss owned by P. Hawksfield and son.

Position of the *U-16*   51°- 08′- 40N.   01°- 28′- 30E.
U-Boat. Built in 1936 by Deutsche Werke AG, Kiel. Length 140 feet. Beam 13 feet. 279 tons. At time of loss owned by the German Navy.

Position of the *MAHRATTA*   51°- 14′- 45N.   01°- 28′- 85E.
Steam ship. Built in 1913 by R.Duncan Co Ltd, Port Glasgow. Length 445 feet. Beam 58 feet. 6690 GRT. At time of loss owned by T and J Brocklebank Ltd.

Position of the *NORA*   51°- 13′- 45N.   01°- 24′- 43E.
Motor vessel. Built in 1931 by N.V.Werf. 'Voorthuit', Enkhuizen. Length 129 feet. Beam 23 feet. 298 GRT. At time of loss owned by Moats – Zeeuwsch – Vlaanderen.

Position of the *DV-819*   51°-11′- 00N.   01°- 23′- 70E.
Wellington bomber. Built by Vickers-Armstrong, Weybridge. Length 64 feet. Wing span 86 feet. 18,556 lbs. At time of loss owned by the Royal Air Force.

Position of the *MISS LOLLIPOP*   51°- 08′- 52N.   01°- 24′- 10E.
B17g aircraft. Built 1944 by Lockheed, Burbank. Length 74 feet. Wing span 103 feet. 65,500 lbs. At time of loss owned by United States Air Force.

Position of the *NANCY MORAN*   51°- 09′- 61N.   01°- 27′- 82E.
Steam tug. Built 1912 at Staten Island S.B Co, New Jersey. Length 144 feet. Beam 29 feet. 452 GRT. At time of loss owned by United States War Administration.

Position of the *LURAY VICTORY*   51°- 11′- 04N.   01°- 31′- 62E.
Steam ship. Built in 1944 by Californian Shipbuilding Corp, L.A. Length 439 feet. Beam 62 feet. 7,612 GRT. At time of loss owned by Black Diamond Steamship Co.

Position of *NORTH EASTERN VICTORY*   51°- 12′- 38N.   01°- 32′- 42E.
Steam ship. Built in 1945 by Permanente Metals Corporation, California. Length 439 feet. Beam 62 feet. 7,612 GRT. At time of loss owned by Lyke Line.

Position of *SILVIA ONORATO*   51°- 12′- 53N.   01°- 33′- 04E.
Steam ship. Built in 1916 by J. Priestman & Co, Sunderland. Length 290 feet. Beam 40 feet. 2,327 GRT. At time of loss owned by Achille Onorato.

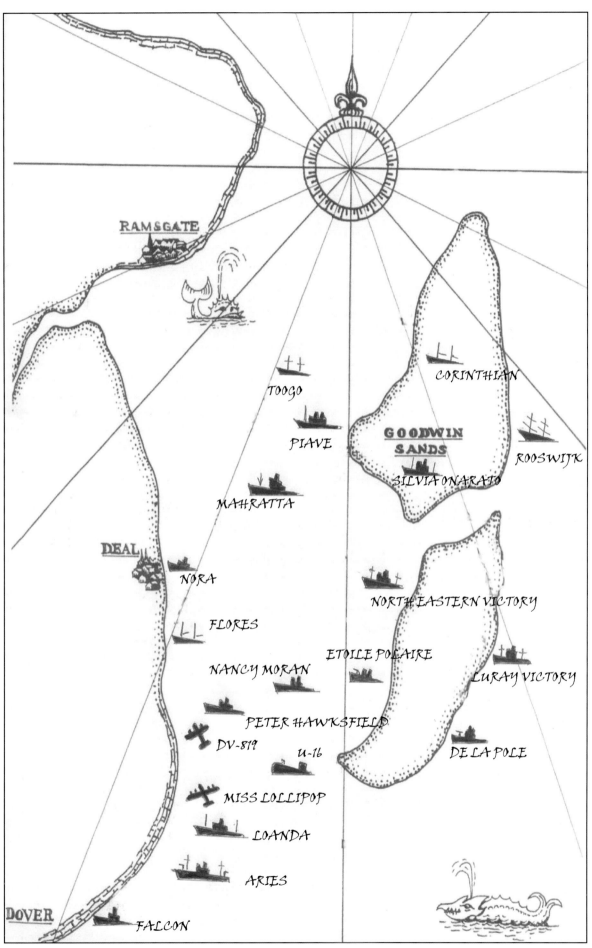

RAMSGATE

TOOGO

PIAVE

CORINTHIAN

GOODWIN
SANDS

ROOSWIJK

SILVIA ONARATO

MAHRATTA

DEAL

NORA

NORTH EASTERN VICTORY

FLORES

ETOILE POLAIRE

NANCY MORAN

LURAY VICTORY

PETER HAWKSFIELD

DE LA POLE

DV-819

U-16

MISS LOLLIPOP

LOANDA

ARIES

DOVER

FALCON

ACKNOWLEGMENTS

My wife Hazel and daughter Emma for being enthusiastic, patient and helping me to make the stories, hopefully, readable. My thanks to the lovely Lesley Daley, for proof reading and giving me encouragement – being a Deal boatman for forty years most of my adjectives and grammar are pure Anglo Saxon. Skipper Allan Booth, a good friend, for looking over my shoulder and giving me a nudge in the right direction. Underwater explorer Bob Peacock, who is finding more Goodwin Sands shipwrecks than I can put names to. Martin Phillips, a great angler with an academic brain. Les Coe, Walmer Lifeboat station. Gerry Dowd and John Maxted, divers, whose illustrations helped complete a little known story. The dedication and daring of Ken Welling. A blast from the past, Pete Orrill for a much wanted photo. Deal Maritime Museum, a place well worth a visit. The East Kent Mercury archives, held at Deal Library. Tom Burnham, for use of his chart. World Ship Society, essential for the serious researcher. The staff at Deal Library for being so obliging. Dennis Wells, Tartan Hedgehog Printing Services, helpful and professional.

Bibliography:

'Seamen of the Downs' (1929), Bayley, G. B.
'Keeper of the gate' Iron, J.Captain.
'Life on a Lightship' Cooke, A.O.
'The Goodwin Sands' (1953), Goldsmith-Carter, G.
'The Dover Patrol 1915-1917' (1932), Bacon, R. Admiral. K.C.B., K.C.V.O.
'The Piccadilly of the Sea – St. Margaret's Bay' (1910), Harris Stone, J.
'Dive Kent' (1994), McDonald, Kendall.
'Tales from around the Goodwin Sands' (2004), Chamberlain, D.
'The Big Barges'(1983), Benham, H. Finch, R.

Glossary:

Clagg.	Cold mist
Flaking	Laying out untangled rope on the deck
Haul-off rope	A thick rope anchored sea-ward to help pull the lifeboat off
Jacob's ladder	Rope ladder with hard-wood foot-slats
Samson Post.	An oak post to secure the anchor rope
Scoot.	A small Dutch coaster
Sea Dive.	Acronym for South East Archaeological Divers
Swatch-way.	A passageway through the Goodwin Sands
Swaddled	A ship sinking into the Goodwin Sands
Three-Pounder	Deck gun
12 Pounder	Deck gun